THE RESPONSIBILITY OF HERMENEUTICS

by

ROGER LUNDIN

ANTHONY C. THISELTON

CLARENCE WALHOUT

WILLIAM B. EERDMANS PUBLISHING COMPANY
THE PATERNOSTER PRESS

Copyright © 1985 by Wm. B. Eerdmans Publishing Co.

William B. Eerdmans Publishing Company
255 Jefferson Ave. S.E., Grand Rapids, Mich. 49503

and

The Paternoster Press Ltd.
3 Mount Radford Crescent, Exeter EX2 4JW, England

Library of Congress Cataloging-in-Publication Data

Lundin, Roger.
 The responsibility of hermeneutics.

 1. Hermeneutics. 2. Bible—Hermeneutics. 3. Jesus
Christ—Parables. I. Thiselton, Anthony C. II. Walhout,
Clarence, 1934-   III. Title.
BD241.L86 1985   121'.68   85-16132

ISBN 0-8028-0029-7

British Library Cataloguing in Publication Data

Walhout, Clarence
 The responsibility of hermeneutics.
 1. Hermeneutics
 I. Title   II. Lundin, Roger   III. Thiselton,
Anthony C.
 121'.68   BD241

ISBN 0-85364-408-X

CONTENTS

ACKNOWLEDGMENTS

This book embodies results of collaboration and research made possible solely through the vision and financial generosity of the Calvin Center for Christian Scholarship of Calvin College, Grand Rapids, Michigan. The authors were appointed as Fellows of the Center for the year 1982-1983. We represent different academic disciplines and bring together experiences from different institutions, but we share a common commitment to the Christian faith as expressed in Reformed traditions and a common conviction concerning the importance and relevance of hermeneutics for our disciplines and for Christian thought.

We wish to express our gratitude to the Governing Board of the Calvin Center for making possible this venture in collaborative Christian scholarship. This year's work achieved more results for our thinking and writing than appear within the confines of this book, but the present volume represents one tangible product. We wish to express our thanks not only for financial support during the project but also for assistance in a variety of ways, including consultations with other scholars.

Our thanks go also to a number of academic colleagues. We cannot mention them all by name, but we owe a particular debt to Professor Henry Vander Goot and to Professor David Hoekema who served as Fellows with us and shared many of our discussions, and also to Professor Nicholas Wolterstorff whose writings and oral comments were stimulating and constructive at numerous points. Our secretary, Mrs. Nell Tjapkes, worked patiently and generously not only in typing the final manuscript but also in typing other papers, some of which may see publication elsewhere. Together with her, we also wish to thank our publishers for their help and supportive concern. We owe a special debt to Mr. Jon Pott and Mr. Charles Van Hof of William B. Eerdmans Publishing Company for seeing our work safely through the press.

February 1985

ROGER LUNDIN
ANTHONY C. THISELTON
CLARENCE WALHOUT

INTRODUCTION

Hermeneutics is a fashionable term in biblical and literary studies, but for many people it also raises suspicions. These suspicions stem only partly from the faddishness of the label. They arise also because the subject seems to promise so much and to deliver so little.

In this volume we suggest that contemporary discussions of hermeneutics have become either overly polemical or disappointingly unproductive because of the exhaustion of our traditional interpretive models. Often our common terms, such as *validity, meaning, correctness, application, subjectivity,* and *objectivity,* carry with them certain assumptions that dictate the course of the discussion. In order to view the subject afresh, we have tried to explore new models for interpretation, and have been drawn especially to those built upon concepts of action and responsibility. We believe it essential to acknowledge that speaking and writing and interpreting are human actions that arise within specific contexts. When we view the composing and interpreting of texts as actions or sequences of actions, we are more likely to introduce the concept of responsibility into hermeneutics than when we are concerned only with correctness or validity. To compose and to interpret texts is to engage in responsible action.

The literature on the subject of hermeneutics often implies that what makes interpretation so important is our human desire to know the truth. And often it is assumed that our goal is to achieve a single correct interpretation because the truth cannot accommodate conflicting views. We wish to claim, however, that no less fundamental than the question of truth is the question of ethics; no less fundamental than our concern for true knowledge is our concern for right action. Because understanding is itself an action or a sequence of actions, it is closely related to all of our other actions and the purposes we have for them. We organize our activities in relation to the goals we want to achieve, and the means we use to reach those goals reveal what we regard as responsible action.

In ordinary circumstances questions of ethics and responsibility can appear so distant from the problems of interpreting texts as to seem irrelevant. The failure, however, to acknowledge the role of ethics in hermeneutics accounts for much of the strife we discover in the history of interpretation. Anyone who investigates conflicts in interpretation, for example, will discover debates in which the issue is not really the interpretation itself but the nature of the interpreter's goals or the effects of a given interpretation on a community of people who have an interest in the text being interpreted. Bias, acrimony, censorship, and emotional recrimination are perhaps the most evident in religious communities where the meaning of a sacred text has a special importance, but such "ethical," or in many cases "moralistic," debates have also colored and complicated hermeneutical conflicts in academic communities. However, modern educated people tend to be put off by "moralism" and attempt to separate ethics and hermeneutics. Literary critics, for example, have often made disclaimers about the ethical implications of their work; in the discipline of literary studies aesthetic criticism is often distinguished from moral reflection. John Crowe Ransom phrased this view characteristically when he asserted that while literary criticism is not unethical, it is "post ethical."[1]

In biblical studies, too, a sharp division has emerged between those who believe that biblical "sciences" are free of questions of value and those who believe that a prior "faith" attitude is a necessary hermeneutical principle. An exploration of the critique of action and responsibility may perhaps serve to carry this discussion forward more constructively. Hermeneutics is not simply a cognitive process whereby we determine the "correct meaning" of a passage or text. Questions of truth and universality are important, but so are questions of cultural value and social relevance. Because the interpretation of texts cannot avoid the historical contexts and actions of both authors and interpreters, questions of ethics and responsible interpretation are as germane to hermeneutics as questions of validity and correctness.

Anyone who studies the history of interpretation may well sympathize with those in the modern age who seek to separate ethics and hermeneutics. The muddled and occasionally harmful mixture of the two can tempt us to desire a clean break between them. To separate them, however, is to sever the ties between two things inescapably bound together. Instead of attempting to isolate ethics and hermeneutics, we should strive to understand the relationship between them.

We can in large part attribute the tendency to separate ethics and hermeneutics to the Cartesian and Kantian traditions which constitute our primary philosophical inheritance. Kant's sharp distinction between pure reason and aesthetic thought has nurtured the common assumption that hermeneutics deals with what can be rationally and disinterestedly asserted about the meaning of texts and that the value of texts for our communal lives is a matter of aesthetic or ethical appropriation. This habit of thought is discussed at some length in the opening section of this book. Throughout the book we adopt a stance which avoids commitment to a distinctively Kantian viewpoint.

The interpretation of texts might not, of course, and need not, determine behavior directly; in fact, it is better to conceive of behavior and responsibility as the context within which formal understanding is pursued. Yet understanding does exist in a reciprocal relationship to behavior, and the importance of hermeneutics is precisely that interpretations influence actions even as actions establish the contexts within which interpretations are made. What is at stake in hermeneutics is not only the *truth* of one's interpretation but also the effects interpretation and interpretive strategies have on the ways in which human beings shape their goals and their actions. These effects may be indirect and they may be filtered through layers of academic discussion and cultural prejudice, but the difference they make is to be seen in the final analysis in their role, small or large, in the shaping of human actions. If it were not so, we would care little about how anyone interpreted a novel or a sacred scripture.

I

OUR HERMENEUTICAL INHERITANCE

Roger Lundin

HERMENEUTICS HAS TO DO WITH INTERPRETATION. On that, at least, almost all who have sought to define the word would agree. And because it deals with interpretation, it involves a study of texts—literary works, the Bible, and works of art—and those who seek to understand such texts.[1] In succeeding chapters we will examine some of the theoretical dimensions of contemporary hermeneutical thinking and will discuss specific questions of biblical interpretation while exploring hermeneutics and the parables of Jesus.

But before we begin to consider historical developments in hermeneutical thinking, impasses in hermeneutical practice, and responses to contemporary perspectives, we should listen to two figures from the past tell us about their own habits of reading and interpreting. In this way we may gain insights into the reading process and an entry into our theoretical discussion. As we listen to these readers, we may do well to ask ourselves which one we would be more likely to trust, admire, and seek to emulate.

Our first reader is an intense and volatile man. Having led a restless and often dissolute life as a young man, he now finds himself unsatisfied and in search of spiritual comfort. At a moment of supreme spiritual crisis, he overhears the snippet of a phrase uttered by a young child. Inspired by this phrase to read the Scriptures, he grabs a Bible, opens it, scans the first passage he finds, hears God's truth in it, and discovers in that moment the seeds of a lifetime of change and regeneration:

> I flung myself down on the ground somehow under a fig tree and . . . kept saying to you, not perhaps in these words, but with this sense: *"And Thou, O Lord, how long? How long, Lord; wilt Thou be angry forever? Remember not our former iniquities."* For I felt that it was these which were holding me fast. And in my misery I would exclaim: "How long, how long this 'tomorrow and tomorrow'? Why not now? Why not finish this very hour with my uncleanness?"

> So I spoke, weeping in the bitter contrition of my heart. Suddenly a voice reaches my ears from a nearby house. It is the voice of a boy or a girl (I don't know which) and in a kind of singsong the words are constantly repeated: "Take it and read it. Take it and read it!" . . . I checked the force of my tears and rose to my feet, being quite certain that I must interpret this as a divine command to me to open the book and read the first passage which I should come upon. For I had heard this about Antony: he had happened to come in when the Gospel was being read, and as though the words read were spoken directly to himself, had received the admonition: *Go, sell all that thou hast, and give to the poor, and thou shalt have treasure in heaven, and come and follow me.* And by such an oracle he had been immediately converted to you.

> So I went eagerly back to the place where Alypius was sitting, since it was there that I had left the book of the Apostle when I rose to my feet. I snatched up the book, opened it, and read in silence the passage upon which my eyes first fell: *Not in rioting and drunkenness, not in chambering and wantonness, not in strife and envying: but put ye on the Lord Jesus Christ, and make not provision for the flesh in concupiscence.* I had no wish to read further; there was no need to. For immediately I had reached the end of this sentence it was as though my heart was filled with a light of confidence and all the shadows of my doubt were swept away.[2]

When facing a text or any object, our other reader seeks to remove from his mind all impediments and prejudices. When confronting a text, he wants to examine it in the same way he explores his world and his self. He wants to approach it methodically, taking nothing for granted and granting nothing to any authority, tradition, or inclination that might seek to influence his judgment before he encounters the object of his study. Though the following passage does not speak specifically about the act of reading, its understanding of the human subject was to prove of great significance for modern theories of interpretation:

> It is now several years since I first became aware how many false opinions I had from my childhood been admitting as true, and how doubtful was everything I have subsequently based on them. Accordingly I have ever since been convinced that if I am to establish anything firm and lasting in the sciences, I must once and for all, and by a deliberate effort, rid myself of all those opinions to which I have hitherto given credence, starting entirely new, and building from the foundation up.

Our "reader" goes on to describe the way in which his fear of the size of the task has kept him from attempting to undertake it. But now, he realizes, he must make the effort:

> Today, then, as I have suitably freed my mind from all cares, and have secured for myself an assured leisure in peaceful solitude, I shall at last apply myself earnestly and freely to the general overthrow of all my former opinions. In doing so, it will not be necessary for me to show that they are one and all false; that is perhaps more than can be done. But since reason has already persuaded me that I ought to withhold belief no less carefully from things not entirely certain and indubitable than from those things which appear to me manifestly false, I shall be justified in setting all of them aside, if in each case I can find any ground whatsoever for regarding them as dubitable. Nor in so doing shall I be investigating each belief separately—that, like inquiry into their falsity, would be an endless labour. The withdrawal of foundations involves the downfall of whatever rests on these foundations, and what I shall therefore begin by examining are the principles on which my former beliefs rested. . . .
>
> But it may be said, although the senses sometimes deceive us regarding minute objects, or such as are at a great distance from us, there are yet many other things which, though known by way of sense, are too evident to be doubted; as, for instance, that I am in this place, seated by the fire, attired in a dressing-gown, having this paper in my hands, and other similar seeming certainties.[3]

Many will recognize these two readers as St. Augustine and René Descartes. When we ask which one we would be most likely to trust, admire, and seek to emulate, we may very well have reservations about the approach to the scriptural text taken by Augustine. Admittedly arbitrary, Augustine's way of dealing with the Scriptures seems shaped more by whim than anything else. As such, it is the kind of approach that few who wish to read with rigor and precision will claim to have adopted. And yet even as we question Augustine's practice, we can see in it many of our own habits. Our deepest sympathies very likely lie more with Augustine and our actual practices resemble his, while our theory demands that we think of the pursuit of truth in the way Descartes seems to do. We live as Augustine and dream we're Descartes. And that fact is one of the main sources of our confused notions about hermeneutics.

The Cartesian and Baconian Legacies

Descartes serves as a particularly instructive example, because Cartesian assumptions have done much to shape our theories about the interpretation of the Bible, literary texts, and works of art. If he is "to establish anything firm and lasting in the sciences," Descartes argues, the scientist, philosopher, or critic must "by a deliberate effort" rid himself of all preconceived notions and start entirely anew, "building from the foundations up." Cartesian doubt seeks to peel away the layers of tradition which keep the self from direct contact with the world. As we shall see, this provocative assumption—that we get at truth by setting aside all our assumptions—lies at the heart of a great deal of theorizing about interpretation in the modern world. And it is this belief which several recent theorists have questioned dramatically.

Once he has discarded all, thrown all into doubt, Descartes still finds some ideas so self-evidently persuasive that he recognizes them as clear and certain truths. In this context Descartes propounds his now famous dictum: *cogito ergo sum.* One thing he cannot doubt: that he, who is doing the doubting, must exist. Otherwise, he could not be doubting his own existence. Then, once he has established the point that he exists, Descartes proceeds to claim to prove the existence of both God and the external world. But the price paid for such certainty appears high. Assurance about the self and God (and the external world) seems intertwined with self-conscious awareness. Only because I think and am self-consciously aware of that fact can I be sure that I exist and am I enabled to deduce innumerable other truths about the world and my experiences in it. "Descartes paves the way for making the relevance of the knowing self the center of thought," the German theologian Helmut Thielicke claims. "Henceforth every object of thought, understanding, perception, and indeed will and belief, is related to the conditions contained for these acts in the subject that executes them. . . . Man, then, always stands over against what he observes; he is always himself a theme."[4]

Superficially at least, the deductive method of Cartesian rationalism would seem at odds with another school of thought prominent in the seventeenth and eighteenth centuries, that of Baconian inductive science. Francis Bacon stressed the need for a rigorous empirical examination of physical, historical, and experiential data. The observer was to study the data before him without allowing his biases to shape the organization of the facts. Once he had done so, Bacon claimed, the laws governing those facts would reveal themselves to him. Bacon particularly disparaged what he called the four "idols" that impeded man in his quest for certain knowledge. The "Idols of the Tribe" are misguided human beliefs in the total reliability of sense perception; the "Idols of the Cave" are our habits of valuing our private and particular understandings of experience too highly; "Idols of the Market" have to do with the ambiguity and imprecision of human language; and finally, the "Idols of the Theater" lead us to accept unthinkingly the dogmas handed down through tradition. The only antidote for the poisonous influence of these idols was the painstaking study of facts.[5]

Bacon saw himself as an intellectual explorer making a decisive break with tradition. In imagery that is particularly significant in an American context, he likened himself to Columbus. He thought of himself as an explorer in search of a "new intellectual world" who would "sail through the Pillars of Hercules, symbol of the old world, into the Atlantic Ocean of new discovery."[6] To an explorer studying the facts of the present, the past could bring little of use; indeed, the voyage into a future of material gain and increased power would only be slowed, or even halted, as long as the ship of inductive discovery remained anchored to antiquity.

Despite their apparent dissimilarities, the Baconian and Cartesian methods share certain assumptions. And though we cannot trace every later development back to Descartes and Bacon, the rationalism and empiricism they espoused did significantly shape the Enlightenment and, through the Enlightenment, many modern attitudes about the role of tradition and the place of history in human life. As one student of the history of ideas has observed: "The deduction from all this, from both Baconian and Cartesian science, was that the present knew better than the past, that there was simply no comparison between past and present as to correct thinking, or as to solid knowledge."[7]

In *Truth and Method,* his study of hermeneutical theory, Hans-Georg Gadamer examines the pervasiveness of Cartesianism in the Enlightenment tradition in the West. "The fundamental prejudice of the enlightenment is the prejudice against prejudice itself, which deprives tradition of its power," Gadamer argues.[8] Modern science follows both "the rule of Cartesian doubt of accepting nothing as certain which can in any way be doubted, and the idea of method that adheres to this requirement."[9] Many modern theories of interpretation embrace Cartesianism when they denigrate the role of tradition in interpretation and seek indubitable methods to employ in the understanding of the Bible, historical actions, and literary texts. As heirs of Cartesianism, we find that though our experience seems to indicate that we read as Augustine reads—as people who seek the truth, who are profoundly interested in that truth, and who belong to communities whose traditions mediate our understanding of what we read—we dream in our theory that we act like Descartes—that our reading of the Bible, of a novel, or the actions of an individual or group can be a totally disinterested, scientific affair.

The Cartesian approach, especially as it has been assimilated and transmitted by the Enlightenment tradition, has extended its dominion over so much of modern thought that even when certain groups—such as the romantic poets and various orthodox Christians—have protested its encroachments, they have largely done so in the language of the Cartesian theoretical kingdom in which they unwittingly dwell.

The Cartesian Isolation of the Aesthetic Category

It is indeed ironic that at the very time that Cartesian and Baconian foundations have been called into profound question, a number of aestheticians and theologians, as disturbed as they are by elements in the Enlightenment legacy, have only clung more tightly to Baconianism and Cartesianism. The list of those who have offered a sharp challenge to the Cartesian tradition is impressive: Martin Heidegger and Hans-Georg Gadamer in philosophical hermeneutics and aesthetic theory, Max Black and Paul Ricoeur in the theory of metaphor, Ludwig Wittgenstein and J. L. Austin in the study of the functions of language, and Thomas Kuhn and Stephen Toulmin in the philosophy of science. Though this is a disparate group, its members share a desire to rethink some of our most basic notions about texts, interpreters, and language.

To understand the problems several of these theorists address, we can examine the development of one particular discipline of thought—aesthetic theory—over the past several centuries. In recent years scholars have closely scrutinized the historical background of aesthetic beliefs that many in the West have long taken for granted. In an essay "On the Origins of 'Aesthetic Disinterestedness,' " Jerome Stolnitz traces one central modern doctrine back to debates in the field of ethical theory in the seventeenth and eighteenth centuries, the era of Descartes and Bacon and of their growing influence. It was the Earl of Shaftesbury who introduced the term "disinterestedness" into discussions of ethics and the arts. He did so, in part, to counter the egoism of seventeenth-century empiricism, especially the empiricism of Thomas Hobbes, which claimed that self-love and the instinct for self-preservation grounded all human actions. By arguing forcefully against the possibility of disinterested human action, Hobbes seemed to deny, at least in the sphere of ethics, the feasibility of a Cartesian model of detached observation and reflection.

Viewing empiricist notions as a threat to religious belief and moral purity, Shaftesbury sought to argue that "genuine moral and religious concern are with what is intrinsic and that they are therefore terminal. They are not instrumental and therefore anticipatory." One who has a truly virtuous love of God will refuse to entertain questions about rewards and punishments and will worship him solely for his own sake. Rather than being a matter of choosing and acting as an imperfect agent in an imperfect world, ethics for Shaftesbury became at its highest level an affair of "loving" the "view or contemplation" of virtue.[10]

On the surface of things, such eighteenth-century discussions of ethical virtue might seem unrelated to contemporary controversies over the interpretation of the Bible and literary texts. But though modern aesthetic theory appears to be a tapestry of many colors, a few strong threads hold its theoretical fabric together. And one of these, the doctrine of aesthetic disinterestedness, was spun on the wheel of ethical reflection almost three hundred years ago. As Stolnitz explains, over the course of the eighteenth century the doctrine of ethical disinterestedness began to be applied to what we now call the "fine arts." In fact the theory of disinterestedness had a good deal to do with the consolidation of our modern definition of those arts. The "fine" were opposed to the "useful" arts. The useful arts involved the creation of tools to be employed by human agents in action—hymns to be sung as acts of praise to God or pots to be used in the preparation of food. The fine arts, however, were to serve no end greater than themselves; they were, like God and the good, to be studied, admired, and worshiped in and of themselves and not as means to any other ends. Like any object in a Cartesian scheme of subject-object dualism, the work of art was to be examined with detachment and precision. And the moral difference between "fine" and "applied" arts was this: while human beings pursued the study of nature with the aims of mastery and use in mind, they were to cultivate the appreciation of the arts with no other end in sight than that of disinterested delight.[11]

As he did in so many areas of thought, Immanuel Kant con-
solidated, synthesized, and reformulated dominant aesthetic beliefs
at the end of the eighteenth century. Kant, whose influence upon
later aesthetic theory would be great, took exception to Shaftesbury's
and Francis Hutcheson's linking of moral and aesthetic judgments.
According to Kant the delight an individual takes in what is agreeable
and good is always tinged with self-interest:

> This is true, not alone of the agreeable and the mediately good,
> i.e., the useful, which pleases as a means to some pleasure, but
> also is true of that which is good absolutely and from every
> point of view, namely the moral good which carries with it the
> highest interest. For the good as the object of will, and taking
> an interest in it, are identical.[12]

Yet Kant believed that in one realm, the aesthetic,
disinterestedness remained a possibility. *"Taste* is the faculty," Kant
claimed in his *Critique of Judgment,* "for estimating an object or
a mode or representation by means of a delight or aversion *apart
from any interest.* The object of such a delight is called *beautiful.* "[13]

Kant sought to do two things with taste. First, he wanted to
argue that judgments of taste are not solipsistic but intersubjective.
Because an individual's delight in an aesthetic object is not, at least
in theory, tied to any "interest" in that object, the individual must
regard his free, untainted, and uncoerced enjoyment "as resting on
what he may also presuppose in every other person. . . . The judgment of taste, with its attendant consciousness of detachment from
all interest, must involve a claim to validity for all men,
and . . . there must be coupled with it a claim to subjective universality."[14]

At the same time that he was claiming a "subjective universality" for a proper response to a work of art, Kant was clearly
distinguishing between imaginative knowing and other forms of
knowledge. He argued that "the judgment of taste . . . is not a
cognitive judgment, and so not logical, but is aesthetic—which means
that it is one whose determining ground *cannot be other than subjective.* "[15] Unlike some—especially Ralph Waldo Emerson and those
influenced by him—who would attempt to use Kant's insights as the
basis for a radical romantic idealism, Kant himself was very clear
about the limits of art. Stressing its "disinterested" nature, he labeled
the aesthetic experience as the subjective "feeling of purposiveness
without the idea of purpose" and distinguished its activity from the
processes involved in rational conceptualization and scientific
discovery.

Developed by Hutcheson, Edmund Burke, Kant, Arthur Schopenhauer, and others, this line of thinking did much to shape the romantic movement at the end of the eighteenth century. In fact, what we might call romantic formalism—an approach that has prevailed in literary study in the West for almost two hundred years—came into being in England and on the Continent in the closing decades of that century. We find in the thought of that time the shaping of most of the aesthetic assumptions we have until recently taken for granted—such things as the isolation and subsequent exaltation of the aesthetic category, the sharp distinction between poetic discourse and all other forms of discourse, the granting of primacy to formal criteria in the evaluation of the work of art, the denial of art's didactic functions and the concomitant celebration of its ability to give pleasure, and the emphasis upon the self-contained, nonreferential, sacred nature of the work itself.

We might see romantic formalism as Cartesianism set in large type or painted on a very broad canvas. It is not that the romantic poets and their heirs shared with Descartes a faith in the supreme value of the disinterested search for truth undertaken with the aid of reason and methodological rigor. In fact, the romantics repeatedly defined themselves over against rationalism and the scientific method. But in thus defining themselves, those who work within the romantic tradition have generally not questioned the right or power of "science" or "reason" to describe and order certain kinds of reality. In essence they have accepted the Cartesian picture of the self's place in the world and have simply opposed to the truths of science the affective truths of the human spirit. Romantic theory has tended to claim both that art deals largely, if not exclusively, with that body of affective truths and that those truths are distinct from and in some ways even superior to scientific truths. What Thielicke calls the Cartesian "knowing self" remains as much "the center of thought" in romantic and postromantic art as it has been in various other philosophical and theological systems of recent centuries.

What we find in romanticism is a Cartesianism of the imagination. Much recent scholarship has stressed the way in which the romantic movement attempted to salvage Judeo-Christian values by appropriating for the individual consciousness powers and prerogatives formerly assigned to God in Christian theism. In his study of the period, M. H. Abrams argues that romantic writers undertook

> to save traditional concepts, schemes, and values which had been based on the relation of the Creator to his creature and crea-

tion, but to reformulate them within the prevailing two-term
system of subject and object, ego and non-ego, the human mind
or consciousness and its transactions with nature.[16]

As Abrams demonstrates, our traditional beliefs about romanticism are accurate as far as they go: it was a reaction against the
mechanistic and rationalistic tendencies of the Enlightenment; it was
an attempt to counter the burgeoning power of science and in-
dustrialization; and it was an effort to reassert the place of the passions and intuition in human affairs. But we have largely neglected
until recently the revolutionary nature of its program to reconstitute
traditional belief. We have also frequently failed to note the continuity between the Cartesianism of the Enlightenment and the
romantic rebellion against the rationalistic elements of the Enlightenment. One way to assess romanticism, especially in Germany,
England, and America, is to view it as a form of radical Protestantism, whose goal we can see quite clearly in a portion of the poem
Wordsworth published as a "Prospectus" to an epic *(The Recluse)*
he never finished:

> Paradise, and groves
> Elysian, Fortunate Fields—like those of old
> Sought in the Atlantic Main, why should they be
> A history only of departed things,
> Or a mere fiction of what never was?
> For the discerning intellect of Man
> When wedded to this goodly universe
> In love and holy passion, shall we find these
> A simple produce of the common day.[17]

We find embedded in the images of this passage many of the
assumptions of the romantic poetic and critical traditions. We see
nostalgia for an Eden that was lost long ago or perhaps never existed at all, and frustration with a theological system that either asks
us to postpone our expectations or tricks us into believing in a Beginning that never was and an End that will never be. One notes also
the implications of the sexual imagery used to describe the relationship of the "discerning intellect" (the Kantian "Reason" or the Cole-
ridgian "Imagination") to nature. In typical romantic fashion,
Wordsworth makes the imaginative "intellect" a male principle
which unites with and seeds the passive, female principle of nature
("this goodly universe"). Out of what Wordsworth later in the poem
calls "this great consummation" will come a paradise that is "a
simple produce of the common day."

In the early days of the romantic movement—the decade of the

1790s when many English and German romantic artists were coming into their maturity—the examples of the American and French revolutions seemed to promise nothing less than the imaginative, apocalyptic regeneration of historical life. Listing a series of English and German works of the time, Abrams finds them all representing "the French Revolution (or else a coming revolution which will improve upon the French model) as the critical event which signals the emergence of a regenerate man who will inhabit a new world uniting the features of a restored paradise and a recovered Golden Age."[18] With the failure of the French Revolution and the coming of Napoleon, however, the dream of a new social order to be wrought by consciousness faded, only to be replaced, especially in romantic poems, by a vision of the imagination's power to provide a saving consolation and delight in the artistic works it creates.[19] This turning from a vision of political regeneration would have profound consequences for aesthetics in succeeding years. The abandonment of a view of art linked to human action would cause many to follow the Kantian lead by accepting aesthetic disinterestedness and establishing a rigid dichotomy between scientific ("useful") knowledge and aesthetic knowledge.

For example, the later Samuel Taylor Coleridge, chastened by the disintegration of revolutionary hopes, defined a poem as "that species of composition, which is opposed to works of science, by proposing for its *immediate* object, pleasure, not truth."[20] We see here the oppositional thinking that would mark so much of the debate about literature in the decades after Coleridge. In what is the decisive strategic retreat of romantic theory, Coleridge and others after him in effect concede the question of truth to philosophic and scientific discourse. They attempt to salvage the imagination by celebrating its power to induce pleasure, promoting poetry as an alternative to the ways of knowing and experiencing offered by science. As a result of this concession, later artists and critics would struggle to find a place for the imagination in the very world from which they had banished it. In one sense, aesthetic theory has been struggling for two centuries to make grand that which it has already rendered trivial.

For the romantic theorists, the influence of Kant, the failure of the French Revolution, and the implications of some of their own beliefs conspired to move them to notions about art that sound very familiar to us. The romantic tradition has held to the present day to its cardinal assumption that art triumphs by working the wonders of the spirit upon the chaos of the world; it makes cohere that which is essentially incoherent. But while the initial romantic impulse had been to view the human imagination as an agent of political liberation, the fully developed theory would concentrate upon the way in which the individual work of art gives beautiful permanence within its form to the ironies and agonies of history.

Coleridge writes of the imagination in *Biographia Literaria* in 1817 that "it dissolves, diffuses, dissipates, in order to re-create; . . . it struggles to idealize and to unify. It is essentially *vital,* even as all objects (*as* objects) are essentially fixed and dead." John Keats, in a letter from the same year, praises that quality which "went to form a Man of Achievement especially in Literature and which Shakespeare possessed so enormously—I mean *Negative Capability,* that is when man is capable of being in uncertainties, Mysteries, doubts, without any irritable reaching after fact & reason." Keats holds up suspended judgment, detachment from ideological commitments and action—disinterestedness, in other words—as the ideal of theory and practice. Emily Dickinson sounds a neo-Kantian theme, in "Essential Oils—are wrung," when she contrasts the life-giving permanence of art to the brutal, decaying powers of nature:

> The General Rose—decay—
> But this—in Lady's Drawer
> Make Summer—When the Lady lie
> In Ceaseless Rosemary—

Dickinson's poems, pressed from experience through suffering and preserved in a drawer or book, will long outlast the beautiful objects of the natural world. The Victorian Walter Pater sharply distinguishes between fact and value and celebrates the artist's ability to transcend "mere fact":

> For just in proportion as the writer's aim, consciously or unconsciously, comes to be the transcribing, not of the world, not of mere fact, but of his sense of it, he becomes an artist, his work *fine* art; . . . All beauty is in the long run only *fineness* of truth, or what we call expression, the finer accommodation of speech to that vision within.

And in the twentieth century, Robert Frost offers us poetry as a fragile bulwark against chaos:

> The figure a poem makes. It begins in delight and ends in wisdom. . . . It runs a course of lucky events, and ends in a clarification of life—not necessarily a great clarification such as sects and cults are founded on, but in a momentary stay against confusion.[21]

In these passages we encounter key notions of the romantic formalist aesthetic. The work of art, that well-crafted poem, short story, novel, or play, becomes the place in which inert nature and chaotic history are brought to life by the unifying human imagination. Somehow, the ability of the imagination to impart beauty to objects creates a restful space for man—a "momentary stay against confusion"—in an otherwise hostile world. In that space one encounters neither the truths of science and philosophy nor any resolution of human dilemmas; instead, one stands in the presence of a paradoxical enshrinement of human ambiguity in a form that lasts because it pleases and pleases because it lasts.

Walter Ong tellingly places what he calls the "doctrine of the poem as a closed field" in historical perspective.[22] After noting John Stuart Mill's well-known distinction between eloquence and poetry— "eloquence is *heard;* poetry is *overheard"*—Ong observes that "earlier, when 'eloquence' would have included poetry as akin to rhetoric, poets wanted desperately to be heard; even when they were not actually competing with one another, they sang to audiences for applause. But not romantic poets, at least in implied principle."[23] Romantic thinking about the duties of the creative subject removes the artist and his art from the untidy arena of dialogue and action. "The doctrine of the poem as a closed field reveals," Ong argues, "the deep romantic roots of the New Criticism. With romanticism, the old agonistic poetic had been replaced by a new doctrine of creativity. The poet is irenic, or at least neutral, uncommitted, free of dialogic struggle with an audience, since for the 'creative' romantic imagination the poem is no longer a riposte but a simple product, an 'object' rather than an exchange."[24] As we will attempt to document, this move from a view of the work of art as a "riposte" to one which sees the work as a "simple produce" represents a shift of signal importance in the history of hermeneutics. We will argue for the need to view texts as objects and instruments of action, rather than as self-contained worlds uncontaminated by the finitude and guilt that mark all human action.

For Northrop Frye, one of the most prominent critics of the past thirty years, the shift from riposte to object is a welcome one. For even though Frye attempts to distance himself from aestheticism by calling for an inductive science of criticism, he appears quite comfortable with the polar oppositions of romantic thinking.[25] "In all literary verbal structures the final direction of meaning is inward," we are told in *Anatomy of Criticism*. "In literature, questions of fact or truth are subordinated to the primary literary aim of producing a structure of words for its own sake." Working upon these assumptions, Frye distinguishes the literary work from all other discourse by defining it as an "autonomous verbal structure."[26] This sounds strikingly like New Critical definitions of the individual work of art, but even more revealing is the comment with which Frye concludes this passage: "In literature, what entertains is prior to what instructs, or, as we may say, the reality-principle is subordinate to the pleasure-principle."[27]

Frye expands the religion of aestheticism, calling for the worship not of the individual work but of the comprehensive world created by the imagination as an alternative to the alienating worlds of everyday life. Because we live in an "environment" (the natural and historical worlds) which is not a desirable "home," the poet's "job is not to describe nature, but to show you a world completely absorbed and possessed by the human mind."[28] Thus, even though these objective worlds of history and science are what Frye calls "true" and "real" worlds, they must be overwhelmed and appropriated by the imperial imagination. As a neo-Kantian, Frye acknowledges the primary purpose and power of literature to be that of imparting pleasure and satisfying the desire for order and beauty. Yet he wants to extend the dominion of this pleasure and the reign of this desire over all of experience. "Literature does not reflect life, but it doesn't escape or withdraw from life either: it swallows it. And the imagination won't stop until it's swallowed everything."[29] In this metaphor of consumption, we see a provocative instance of the making grand of that which has been rendered trivial. Spurned by the world of factuality and in one sense made irrelevant to that world, the literary imagination returns to devour the very world it is reluctant to describe and cannot transform.

We might call Frye's structuralist system—his massive, coherent, verbal universe—a sign of the modern triumph of language and disinterestedness over action in the theory of art. A survey of the literary landscape since the romantic age shows the steady march of critical thinking to this position. Once the retreat from action to pleasure had been made, it was perhaps inevitable that a theory asserting language as the sole domicile of order and meaning would come to be assumed. Even the deconstructors of recent years, for example, lodge meaning in a theory of language. Perhaps the only significant difference is that Frye's vast and stable "verbal structures" become, in the hands of contemporary critics such as Jacques Derrida and Paul de Man, the tents we must pull down each morning as we continue our nomadic flight through the wilderness that is our world. Or, if we recall one of Frye's own metaphors, we might say that in Frye's particular subject-object dualism, the human subject creates an object, the literary universe, which "swallows" that other object which is the world, while in Derrida's deconstructionism, both the text as object and the critical reader as subject are devoured by the principle of textuality, that principle of indeterminacy and instability present in all language.

Baconianism and a New World Hermeneutic

If Cartesian assumptions have strongly influenced aesthetic theorizing since the Enlightenment, then a form of Baconianism has informed the American context in which our artists, literary critics, and biblical exegetes have done their work. But there is a paradox in the cultural background of interpretation in America. Modern hermeneutical theory speaks of the historically situated nature of all interpreters and their interpretations. There is no such thing as an isolated, presuppositionless reading of a text, the hermeneutical theorists argue. All readings take place within communities and start from presuppositions which inform but do not determine the course of each reading.

If one accepts these assumptions, then it would appear natural, indeed necessary, to undertake an examination of the context in which readers have interpreted texts in America. Paradoxically, however, that context is one in which the significance of contexts themselves is downplayed or denied. American culture displays a deep antipathy to the mediating role played in understanding by history, by institutions, and by communities. To explore the history of interpretation in America is to examine a story of varying degrees of disdain for history.

To trace the development of what we might call an American cultural hermeneutic, we need to travel back to the time before the first explorers reached America's shores. "As a state of mind and a dream, America had existed long before its discovery," Gilbert Chinard writes.

> Ever since the early days of Western civilization, people had dreamed of a lost Paradise, of a Golden Age characterized by abundance, absence of war, and absence of toil. With the first accounts of the New World, it was felt that these dreams and yearnings had become a fact, a geographical reality fraught with unlimited possibilities.[30]

To some, America stood as a self-yielding paradise, a garden of earthly delights in which the entangling weeds of European history had never grown. To others, the New World represented the place in which dedicated Puritans were to embark upon their millennial mission. "We shall find that the God of Israel is among us," John Winthrop told those sailing with him toward Massachusetts Bay in

1630, "when ten of us shall be able to resist a thousand of our enemies; when He shall make us a praise and a glory that men shall say of succeeding plantations, 'the lord make it like that of NEW ENGLAND.' For we must consider that we shall be as a city upon a hill.'"[31]

In either view—of America as Eden or of America as the coming New Jerusalem—the past may be a mere impediment or an outright impertinence. The history of the fallen, finite sons and daughters of Adam is not relevant to the estate of these new Adams and Eves set down in the midst of a recovered Eden. Even John Winthrop, good Puritan that he is, holds out something like a perfectionist hope for those who trek to New England. In the same sermon from which we have just quoted, he tells his fellow Puritans that because of Adam's sin

> it comes that every man is born with this principle in him, to love and seek himself only, and thus a man continueth 'til Christ comes and takes possession of the soul and infuseth another principle, love to God and our brother.[32]

Admittedly, Winthrop urgently seeks to hold in check the more radical possibilities latent in this vision of the new Adam, infused with Christ-like love, living in an unsullied land. But for complex reasons, the theological checks of seventeenth-century New England had all but vanished by the time of the Enlightenment in America. Benjamin Franklin, for instance, declared in his *Autobiography* that what the Calvinist Puritans had thought were the binding sins of human pride had become the amendable *errata* of enlightened humankind; the past, with its record of guilt and failure written across it, was but a slate to be wiped clean through diligent human effort. Franklin's contemporary, St. John de Crèvecoeur, celebrated the way in which Americans loosen their confessional ties and adopt an attitude of studied indifference in matters of religion:

> As I have endeavored to show how Europeans become Americans, it may not be disagreeable to show you likewise how the various Christian sects introduced wear out, and how religious indifference becomes prevalent. When any considerable number of a particular sect happen to dwell contiguous to each other, they immediately erect a temple, and there worship the Divinity agreeably to their own peculiar ideas. Nobody disturbs them.[33]

Winthrop's new Adam growing in a covenantal relationship with God through Christ becomes Crèvecoeur's ideal American "leaving behind him all his ancient prejudices and manners" in order to be "melted into a new race of men."[34]

These attitudes are intriguingly similar to the Cartesian approach. In a manner that resembles Descartes's effort to rid himself of all preconceptions, for example, Franklin and Crèvecoeur appear to celebrate both the insignificance of the past and mankind's ability to act unimpeded by it. For them, men and women in America are not defined by the traditions to which they adhere and from which they emerge, but rather by an identity they are to create in a present neatly detached from the past. "The man of the eighteenth century," argues Karl Barth, was "the champion against prejudices and passions, against vice and hypocrisy, ignorance and superstition, intolerance, partiality and fanaticism."[35] For Franklin, Crèvecoeur, and countless others, an American identity is not something to be received but something to be achieved. "Eighteenth century man began to become conscious of his power for science," Barth continues, ". . . and of a capacity for thinking which was responsible to no other authority than himself."[36]

We can detect distinct differences in tone between the Enlightenment and the romantic age, but we also find clear lines of continuity between them. For though the romantics tried to animate what they saw as the moribund forms of eighteenth-century rationalism and mechanistic science, they did so by appropriating both the Enlightenment's view of human power and what Abrams terms the "prevailing two-term system of subject and object, ego and non-ego" that had been bequeathed by Descartes to the age. In American culture the Enlightenment and romantic legacy became mixed with specific elements of a New World vision. For instance, the work of Ralph Waldo Emerson displays a union of romanticism and particular, often radical, American beliefs. "The centuries are conspirators against the sanity and authority of the soul," Emerson informs us, ". . . and history is an impertinence and an injury, if it be anything more than a cheerful apologue or parable of my being and becoming."[37] Furthermore, though "books are the best of things, well used," in the end they are good "for nothing but to inspire."[38] They, the books, inspire us by provoking us to claim the godlike glory that is rightfully ours:

> Familiar as the voice of the mind is to each, the highest merit we ascribe to Moses, Plato, and Milton is, that they set at naught books and traditions, and spoke not what men said but what they thought. . . . In every work of genius we recognize our own rejected thoughts: they come back to us with a certain alienated majesty.[39]

Emerson's "Divinity School Address" clearly shows the implications of such views for a theory of interpretation. Speaking to a group of seniors at Harvard Divinity School in 1838, Emerson attacks the Unitarianism then reigning at Harvard. Orthodox Christians have often criticized the supposedly unprincipled liberalism of Unitarianism, but Emerson finds the Unitarians too conservative, too bound by their few remaining ties to the Christian tradition. "The true Christianity,—a faith like Christ's in the infinitude of man,— is lost," he complains, and it has been replaced by "an exaggeration of the personal, the positive, the ritual."[40] Urging the Divinity School students "to go alone; to refuse the good models, even those most sacred in the imagination of men, and dare to love God without mediator or veil,"[41] Emerson tells them to abandon belief in a fixed revelation transmitted from the past through the Bible and the tradition of the church. Instead, Emerson admonishes these aspiring preachers to plumb the depths of their own imaginations in search of saving insights, because "the need was never greater of new revelation than now."[42]

Emerson seeks here to sever the ties of the interpreting self to all external sources of authority. He has rejected the idea of reading (particularly the reading of the Scriptures) as in any way a determinate thing. Nothing regulates or guides the interpretation of the text, which has become little more than a stimulus for the free-floating response of the creative reader; the text becomes a pretext for the dance of the imaginative spirit upon the grave of the dead letter. But this does not mean, Emerson believes, that interpretive anarchy will prevail once we abandon ourselves to our individual perceptions. Just as the American Adam was to discover innocence at the heart of experience, so the unimpeded reader of texts is to find a deep, latent meaning that all like him can and should discover. "If the single man plant himself indomitably upon his instincts, and there abide, the huge world will come round to him," Emerson promises.[43] "To believe your own thought," to believe, in effect, your own interpretation of a text or event, "to believe that what is true for you in your private heart, is true for all men,—that is genius. Speak your latent conviction, and it shall be the universal sense."[44]

Such, however, was not to prove true in matters of belief or interpretation, as Emerson painfully learned, and as his contemporaries Hawthorne and Melville argued repeatedly in their fiction. In *The Scarlet Letter,* for example, Hawthorne explores the possibilities of an American romantic hermeneutic. The separate characters—Hester Prynne, Roger Chillingworth, Arthur Dimmesdale, the young Pearl, and the Puritan community—focus intently on Hester's "A" throughout the novel. But they never come to share a common interpretation of the symbol. They are not drawn out of their fixed historical prejudices and into a liberating communal vision. Instead, they relentlessly read into the symbol their simple prejudices and spend most of the novel embellishing their basic beliefs. Hester Prynne, the one character who undergoes a significant change in her thinking, seems only to grow more desperate as she realizes the hopelessness of her interpretive situation. The wearing of the "A" has deepened her sense of injustice and her awareness of the bond of sin and frailty uniting mankind. But because she had realized the impossibility of reforming society, Hester "wandered without a clew in the dark labyrinth of mind; now turned aside by an insurmountable precipice; now starting back from a deep chasm. . . . The scarlet letter had not done its office."[45]

We find in *The Scarlet Letter* the makings of a Protestant and romantic nightmare. Two notions—the priesthood of all believers and the doctrine of romantic individualism—are conflated in the experiences of the characters of the novel, as they often have been in the modern world. The confident journey in search of a common romantic truth becomes a desperate ramble through a trackless forest of uncertainty. And even Emerson, that greatest of optimists, would come to doubt the trustworthiness of the romantic compass. After he had experienced several sharp personal and professional setbacks, he lamented the fact that

> souls never touch their objects. An innavigable sea washes with silent waves between us and the things we aim at and converse with. . . .
>
> Dream delivers us to dream, and there is no end to illusion. Life is a train of moods like a string of beads, and, as we pass through them, they prove to be many-colored lenses which paint the world their own hue, and each shows only what lies in its focus.[46]

Emerson's dilemma is one he shares with many American Protestants, particularly those who have sought to hold to a well-defined orthodoxy. On the one hand, these Protestants have liked the sounds of the romantic and Cartesian chords that people like Emerson have been playing; they have found pleasing the stress on the individual, the devaluation of history, and the claim for the need of an unmediated experience of a text. But on the other hand, they have found little they like in the untamed melody produced by the romantic playing of such notes, as they have been frightened by the subjectivity sanctioned in the process.

In search of a method that would allow them to keep the chords while rearranging the score and regulating its performance, evangelical Protestants of Emerson's day—the early and mid-nineteenth century—turned to Scottish Common Sense Realism and Baconian science for help. Recent scholarship has documented the pervasive reach of Common Sense thinking into almost every corner of nineteenth-century American life, and it has also demonstrated the centrality of the Baconian method in everything from laboratory science to the study of the Bible.[47] With its emphasis upon actuality rather than possibility and its serene faith in the universal accessibility of a clear moral law, Scottish Realism served well the needs of the emerging nation. It was a conservative and consolidating force in a society which touted its freedom even as it feared the anarchical possibilities of such freedom. It helped America—as Philip Schaff remarked in 1855—to remain at one and the same time a land where one sees

> no king; no nobility; no privileged class; no aristocracy, except that . . . of character, talent, and wealth; no orders nor titles. . . , no established church; . . . and yet with all this apparent excess of freedom, a universal respect for right and law; deep reverence for Christianity; a conservative spirit; well-ordered government; perfect security of person and property; and great independence, too, towards other nations.[48]

As an epistemological theory Common Sense Realism offered a counter to the corrosive effects of skepticism and idealism. It claimed that the human mind can know some things with certainty and without the need of validation by an outside authority. The mind can be assured of the existence of the external world and other minds, of the continuity of the self's identity over the course of time, of the reliability of memory and the testimony of others, and of the existence of a moral law within all individuals. In short, the basic laws governing moral and physical life can be discerned by all sincere, right-thinking men and women.

As a social theory this set of beliefs provided a burgeoning democracy with a means of controlling its social life without seeming to contradict its most cherished assumptions about tradition and authority. Though many Old World convictions—about such things as the authority of the established church, the social hierarchy, and the validity of tradition—had been overturned in the century and a half leading up to and culminating in the American Revolution, the Declaration of Independence could still claim certain truths to be "self-evident." Those who looked at history superficially might not be able to discover any pattern in the myriad structures of human thought. The Common Sense Realists, however, held that beneath the surface lay a foundation of commonsensical truth. And now in America, they claimed, for the first time in history a people seemed ready to construct a republic of freedom using nothing but their ingenuity, determination, and unadulterated common sense.

In specific matters of biblical interpretation, Common Sense Realism provided for many nineteenth-century American Christians the foundation, while Baconian science gave them the method and materials they needed to build a sturdy house of belief.[49] To get at the meaning of the Bible, they merely employed the inductive techniques exploited with considerable success by the natural scientists. Unlike the idealists and romantics, who were apt to float away with Hegel and Emerson in their rapt reveries, biblical exegetes were to plant their feet firmly on the ground and build with the material of indubitable facts. In his massive *Systematic Theology,* Charles Hodge in 1873 stated flatly that God

> does not teach men astronomy or chemistry, but He gives them the facts out of which those sciences are constructed. Neither does He teach us systematic theology, but He gives us in the Bible the truths which, properly understood and arranged, constitute the science of theology. As the facts of nature are all related and determined by physical laws, so the facts of the Bible are all related and determined by the nature of God and of his creatures. And as He wills that men should study his works and discover their wonderful organic relation and harmonious combination, so it is his will that we should study his Word, and learn that, like the stars, its truths are not isolated points, but systems, cycles, and epicycles, in unending harmony and grandeur.

The "Inductive Method" that Hodge recommends to theologians and exegetes "agrees in everything essential with the inductive method as applied to the natural sciences." The thelogian is to apply that Baconian method to the Bible, a book which "is to the theologian what nature is to the man of science. It is his storehouse of facts," and "in theology as in natural science, principles are derived from facts." As a physical scientist discovers the laws of motion and gravity by meticulously examining the facts of nature, so must the theologian induct or derive "his theory of virtue, of sin, of liberty, of obligation, from the facts of the Bible."[50] Common Sense Realism provided the democratic American believer with a set of universal truths transcending history, and what it failed to provide in the way of details, Baconian science offered through the inductive culling of facts.

As attractive a synthesis as this is, it has raised serious problems for the theory and practice of interpretation in America. This synthesis is itself very much the product of history, specifically the history of the Enlightenment in America, and is not a self-evident set of truths discernible in nature or capable of being gleaned from the pages of Scripture. It is a position which can be supported with reasoned arguments and biblical citations, but it is unquestionably a belief that arises from a specific historical context and not one that we can declare universally apparent.

The synthesis of Common Sense Realism and the inductive method has also led to obvious problems in the life of the church in America. Because it clings to a myth of neutral observation, it can be used to sanction the beliefs of any group, however aberrant, which claims to have discovered the truth of the Scriptures through an exacting study of them. Commenting upon the formation of the Disciples of Christ in the early nineteenth century, for example, Sydney Ahlstrom notes the paradoxical fact that the "campaign for undoing denominationalism was the chief factor in the origination of a new denomination."[51] The Disciples of Christ movement claimed "no creed but the Bible," and argued that "where the Scripture speak, we speak; where the Scriptures are silent, we are silent." Yet in spite of having as their goal the rediscovery of a "primitive Christianity" that would help to establish Christian unity, the Disciples of Christ were not able to build the unified kingdom upon the rock of inductive exploration. As two disillusioned members of the group complained after they had left it:

> The Bible was the only Confession of our Faith, without any statement of the manner in which we understood even its first principles; therefore no man could be tried, or judged heretic, who professed faith in the scriptures, however heterodox he might be in his sentiments.[52]

And after having surveyed the sectarian landscape of nineteenth-century America, John W. Nevin plaintively asked:

> But what are we to think of it when we find such a motley mass of protesting systems, all laying claim so vigorously here to one and the same watchword? If the Bible be at once so clear and full as a formulary of Christian doctrine and practice, how does it come to pass that where men are left most free . . . to use it in this way, and have the greatest mind to do so, according to their own profession, they are flung assunder so perpetually in their religious faith, instead of being brought together, by its influence.[53]

Furthermore, the view of science offered by the Baconian model has come under serious, sustained attack in the past half century. The final section of this chapter will explore this matter in greater detail, but for now we can briefly acknowledge the theoretical work done in recent decades on the philosophy of language and science by such figures as Wittgenstein, Black, Kuhn, and Toulmin. Though they disagree among themselves on any number of particular points, these theorists share a crucial assumption: that science itself is a historical discipline and that its systems build upon basic metaphors or paradigms. Because of the omnipresence of metaphor, there is no discourse, not even the discourse of the sciences, that can claim to be completely disinterested and untouched by the reality of human historicity.

This last fact is one that American Christians in the fundamentalist tradition and American literary critics of the New Critical school have been reluctant to admit. For though recent work in philosophical hermeneutics, the philosophy of language, and the history of science has shown that we read as Augustine reads in the passage of the *Confessions,* many of us cling stubbornly to our belief that we can approach a text with Cartesian cleanliness and Baconian precision. In the case of the New Criticism, this has often led to finding in every "great" poem or novel the values and concerns of twentieth-century neoorthodoxy or existentialism and to claiming that uncovering such things is no more than recording the "facts" that are there in the literary work. And in our study of the Bible, this Cartesian confidence has sanctioned our imposition of an unacknowledged Enlightenment tradition upon the text of Scripture. It indeed remains a great irony that in seeking to counter some of the admittedly troubling elements of the Enlightenment legacy, many Christians have uncritically appropriated the vocabulary and a good deal of the perspective of the tradition they so strenuously oppose.

Beyond the First Person

In the final paragraph of *From Descartes to Wittgenstein: A Short History of Modern Philosophy,* Roger Scruton offers the following generalization about many of the matters we have been examining:

> One thing is certain, however. The assumption that there is first-person certainty, which provides a starting-point for philosophical enquiry, this assumption which led to the ra-

tionalism of Descartes and to the empiricism of Hume, to so much of modern epistemology and so much of modern metaphysics, has been finally removed from the centre of philosophy.[54]

In *Truth and Method,* for example, Gadamer has in mind a criticism of the idea of "first-person certainty" when he links what he calls the alienation of aesthetic consciousness in the modern world to a more pervasive form of alienation, that of historical consciousness. Both forms he traces back to the development of Cartesian assumptions in the Enlightenment, whose "global demand" he calls the "overcoming of all prejudices."[55] Driven by what one might term either a desire or a need to ground the Cartesian *cogito* independent of tradition and authority, the Enlightenment, as Gadamer has said, established its "fundamental prejudice . . . against prejudice itself, which deprives tradition of its power."[56] We can describe this as "either a desire or a need" because this shift from the late seventeenth to the early nineteenth century was either a misguided assertion of the autonomy of the self-reflective subject or a sincere attempt, using Abrams's terms, "to save traditional concepts, schemes, and values" by reformulating them within a Cartesian framework.

In either case, Gadamer's historical observation is well-taken and is rich in its implications for hermeneutical theory. In the Enlightenment "prejudice against prejudice," we discover one of the main sources of the formalist and fundamentalist desire to be freed from the restraints of authority and tradition; we also see in it the beginnings of the view of the artist as one whose imaginative independence will develop either a new tradition or an alternative space to be inhabited by those weary of the past; and we find here one of the sources of our tendency to celebrate the ideal of disinterestedness.

The disinterested reader is supposedly free of the constraining prejudices of history. But those prejudices are the very things that Gadamer believes the interpreters of texts and history cannot nor need not be free of as they begin the work of interpretation. "Long before we understand ourselves through the process of self-examination, we understand ourselves in a self-evident way in the family, society and state in which we live," he writes in *Truth and Method.* "That is why the prejudices of the individual, far more than his judgments, constitute the historical reality of his being."[57] Proclaiming his deep indebtedness to Heidegger, Gadamer stresses the way in which all reading and understanding begin with the interpreter in some way already "interested" in that which he or she is trying to comprehend. After Heidegger, Paul Ricoeur argues, the hermeneutical enterprise becomes "not a reflection on the sciences of the spirit, but an explication of the ontological ground on which these sciences may be built,"[58] and the idea of a disinterested interpretation of a literary text becomes an impossible one for hermeneutical theory; "the illusion is not in looking for a point of departure, but in looking for it without presuppositions."[59]

Working with such assumptions Gadamer developed his now familiar idea of the "fusion of horizons." The interpreter begins his or her work by anticipating the discovery of certain things within the text and by having some of these expectations thwarted in the reading of it. In this process of affirmation and denial, what Gadamer terms the fusion of horizons takes place. The "life-worlds" or horizons of the author and interpreter find themselves fused in a concentration upon the object, the thing said or pointed to in the text. The reader expands the horizon of the text by appropriating it in a particular historical situation; this is accomplished by asking of the text questions which "always bring out the undetermined possibilities of a thing."[60] The text in turn questions its readers by challenging and enlarging the anticipatory structures they have brought to it; as they encounter alien elements questioning them through the text, they are forced to revise their assumptions. And out of this process comes the fusion of horizons.

It might be more accurate to describe Gadamer's phenomenological study of understanding as a hermeneutical spiral rather than a hermeneutical circle. The circle mistakenly implies a self-enclosed finality; the image of the spiral captures something of what Gadamer implies by the intimidating phrase *wirkungsgeschichtliches Bewusstsein,* or what the translators of *Truth and Method* term "effective-historical consciousness." The interpretation of a text begins with the reader anticipating certain things on the basis of the tradition from which the reader comes; it proceeds as reader and text question each other and find their horizons fused; and it culminates with the production of a revised interpretation which may become a part of the tradition itself, altering the foreunderstanding that will precede subsequent interpretations of the text.

While ontological questions about the nature of language and the status of tradition seem to dominate Gadamer's phenomenological study of interpretation, the work of Ludwig Wittgenstein concentrates more upon the functions and uses of language in specific contexts of inquiry. In *Philosophical Investigations* Wittgenstein asks us to

> think of the tools in a tool-box: there is a hammer, pliers, a
> saw, a screw-driver, a rule, a glue-pot, glue, nails and screws.
> — The functions of words are as diverse as the functions of
> these objects.[61]

We use the words in many varied ways in the countless "language
games" *(Sprachspiel)* we "play" during our normal round of activities. According to Wittgenstein we gain an understanding of the
meaning of a word, phrase, or text by examining its place in the sur-
roundings of human life and action. "Here the term 'language-*game*'
is meant to bring into prominence the fact that the *speaking* of
language is part of an activity, or a form of life."[62] The tie between
language and life is an intimate one, for "to imagine a language
means to imagine a form of life."[63] Even that most disciplined of
human actions, the regular obeying of rules, only makes sense when
seen as part of the larger scheme of action in human communities:
"To obey a rule, to make a report, to give an order, to play a game
of chess, are *customs* (uses, interpretations)."[64]

Wittgenstein's observations about language raise serious questions about the possibility of discovering an abstract or value-free
foundation for interpretation. To understand the words in a text we
must have a related understanding of human action, "for what makes
language teachable is *its connection with observable regularities in
human behavior.*"[65] In spite of the hold that the myth of the
unbiased, private reader has on the Protestant mind, it is clear, in
Anthony Thiselton's words,

> that concepts like "being redeemed," "being spoken to by
> God," and so on, are made intelligible and "teachable" not
> *on the basis of private existential experience but on the basis
> of a public tradition of certain patterns of behavior.* Just as
> what "pain" means depends upon observable regularities in
> pain-behavior, so what "redemption" means depends on
> observable regularities in redemption-behavior.[66]

"Such is the circle," Paul Ricoeur writes in one of his earliest
hermeneutical studies: "hermeneutics proceeds from a prior
understanding of the very thing that it tries to understand by interpreting it."[67] The theory behind Ricoeur's comment on preunderstanding is similar, though not identical, to the view of hermeneutics
implicit in the maxim of the medieval theologian St. Anselm: *Credo
ut intelligam* (I believe in order to understand). Both run counter
to the prevailing Cartesianism of the modern world. Indeed,
Anselm's formula implies what much philosophical reflection upon
hermeneutics has come to discover. Before there is understanding

of any sort—in the study of sciences, in the reading of a novel or the viewing of a painting, and in the interpretation of the Bible— there must be assumptions. Ricoeur claims that hermeneutical theory gives us "reason to think that the *Cogito* is within being, and not vice versa." And granting that, "the task of the philosopher guided by symbols would be to break out of the enchanted enclosure of consciousness of oneself, to end the prerogative of self-reflection."[68]

Even if we sought to argue that the Cartesian model—as it is employed in the romantic tradition and in much biblical study—is still productive because it yields such interesting readings, the question of its validity would remain. Given the nature of language, is it possible for a prejudice-free, isolated reading of a text to take place? We remind ourselves of Ricoeur's comment that the illusion is not in looking for a point of departure for reflection, but in looking for it without presuppositions. Or, Gadamer argues,

> We are always already biased in our thinking and knowing by our linguistic interpretation of the world. . . . To this extent, language is the real mark of our finitude. It is always out beyond us. The consciousness of the individual is not the standard by which the being of language can be measured.[69]

We all inevitably read as people who seek, belong, and act. We are, that is, "interested" before we begin to read a text and remain active as we read it. We belong, to a great extent through language, to the theological, social, and psychological traditions that have molded us as subjects and without whose mediation we could understand nothing, and we seek the beauty and truth of the world we inhabit and images of the worlds in which we would like to live and of the people we should like to become. Because of the nature of language and the nature of our actions, there is not and cannot be a Cartesian, completely disinterested reading of any text. In reading, as in things of the spirit, there is no finding without seeking. Of course one may well discover things which add to or contradict what one expected to find, but one would discover nothing at all without a search. Or, as Emerson tells us, quoting a proverb, "He that would bring home the wealth of the Indies, must carry out the wealth of the Indies."[70]

To say this is not to argue for a form of determinism, a "you will discover only what you have assumed" theory of reading. To be sure, one of the most challenging things about the reading experience is the way in which texts so often uproot the assumptions of reading subjects. But the very possibility of a reader being changed by a text would depend on that subject's being an active, interested seeker rather than a totally dispassionate recipient. One who reads is not an isolated subject who either worships or endangers the text, but rather a member of several communities whose traditions make possible and mediate one's understanding of that text.

Neither is this to argue that the questions raised by the ideal of objectivity have no place within a theory of reading. If one abandons notions about the falsification and validation of interpretations, then one is left in the seductive but lonely worlds of Stanley Fish's "interpretive communities," in which separate traditions rather arbitrarily constitute texts for their own purposes.[71] There are ways of adjudicating interpretive disputes and of testing the validity of individual interpretations, even though any attempt to agree on a single method or principle of interpretation is destined to fail. Our section on the parables of Jesus will make a similar claim about the need to avoid the extremes of reactionary conservatism, which claims that its "common sense" reading of the Bible represents a precise, scientific study of "what is there," and a radically progressive hermeneutic which abandons the search for truth and delights in a subjective search for relevance in the modern age.

A passage from a study of Martin Luther by Paul Althaus may help us at this point. It seems especially appropriate when we consider that Luther's (and Calvin's) spiritual descendants were to become so enamored of Cartesian notions about objectivity and certainty.

> In this sense then, Scripture is the standard of what can and cannot claim to be good tradition of the church. Since Luther emphatically asserts the validity of this standard, his basic affirmation of the church's tradition cannot be unconditional. Rather, it contains the possibility of disagreement. This "no" to tradition is not a basic and universal "no," but is always spoken in a specific situation and based on Scripture. We cannot, however, avoid such rejection of tradition whenever it cannot be harmonized with Scripture because it obviously contradicts it.[72]

"This 'no' to tradition is not a basic and universal 'no,' but is always spoken in a specific situation and based on Scripture": the tradition grounds the reading and opens up understanding for the individual, while the principle or standard of criticism (in Luther's case, Scripture) provides a check upon that tradition. The distancing from tradition is subsequent to the belonging to it. The reader brings assumptions to the text and searches for certain things in the text; this would seem to be an incontrovertible fact of our experience as interpreters. During the actual reading the reader may find some of those assumptions confirmed, some denied, and others clarified and expanded. A good deal of this process of confirmation, alteration, and expansion takes place in the silent transaction between reader and text; much of it also takes place, one would hope, in a dialogue between the reader and others from the past and present who have interpreted this same text. "The text presents a limited field of possible constructions," Ricoeur claims. "The logic of validation allows us to move between the two limits of dogmatism and skepticism. It is always possible to argue for or against an interpretation, to confront interpretations, to arbitrate between them and to seek agreement, even if this agreement remains beyond our immediate reach."[73]

That, it would seem, is one truth that all who seek to understand hermeneutics would do well to realize. Perfect agreement may remain "beyond our immediate reach," but that is not cause for despair. Like texts themselves and those who seek to understand them, interpretations are a part of history. As such, they have pasts which have shaped them and futures which open before them and beckon them. And as one form of human action, the act of interpreting requires of us the same diligence, trust, and perseverance that all of our responsible actions do.

II

TEXTS AND ACTIONS

Clarence Walhout

THE DISCUSSION UP TO THIS POINT has shown how pervasively our thinking about texts is influenced by epistemological theories which derive from the Cartesian and Baconian "revolution" and which are nurtured by Kantian and romantic traditions of thought. The inadequacies of such epistemologies point up the continuing need for new models. In this section we present in systematic fashion a theory of textuality which is not tied to a distinctly Kantian epistemology. Our discussion concentrates on fictional texts, but the aim is to propose a model which is useful for the interpretation of nonfictional texts as well.[1]

In our day, the discussion of textuality and hermeneutics takes place most frequently within a tradition which views language as the locus of meaning. Language theory has subsumed earlier epistemological debates over subjectivity and objectivity by absorbing them into a philosophy of language. Language in this tradition stands between subject and object without denying either and without setting them over against each other as antinomies. Since subject and object can be conceived only within and by means of language, their relationship, in this view, is contingent upon the mediation of language. It becomes necessary, therefore, to concentrate on the medium of language itself because only in language does whatever exists become discernable and discussable. Thus Paul de Man writes: "Instead of conceiving of the poem's rhetoric as the instrument of the subject, of the object, or of the relationship between them, it is preferable to reverse the perspective and to conceive of these categories as standing in the service of the language that has produced them."[2]

Now from one point of view, to argue that questions about texts are really questions about language is natural, for what else is a text but "a piece of language"? This identification, however, is historically significant, for what has become an axiom of contemporary theorizing is of relatively recent vintage. A comparison of typical statements by late nineteenth- and early twentieth-century literary critics with statements from critics who dominate the theoretical landscape today reveals a gradual shift from a focus on life to a focus on language. One of Matthew Arnold's central dogmas, for example, is that literature is "a criticism of life." Taine, in the introduction to his *History of English Literature,* writes: "It is then chiefly by the study of literature that one may construct a moral history, and advance toward the knowledge of psychological laws, from which events spring." From a different perspective Henry James, too, stresses the grounding of literature in life: "A novel is in its broadest definition a personal, a direct impression of life." Most early twentieth-century poets, even though they may show the influence of a romantic aestheticism, do not conceive of poetry as focused more on language than on life. Robert Frost's view of poetry is that "it begins in delight, it inclines to the impulse, it assumes direction with the first line laid down, it runs a course of lucky events, and ends in a clarification of life." William Carlos Williams announces that there are "no ideas but in things," and Wallace Stevens writes: "The relation of art to life is of the first importance especially in a sceptical age since, in the absence of belief in God, the mind turns to its own creations and examines them, not alone from the aesthetic point of view, but for what they reveal, for what they validate and invalidate, for the support that they give." What gradually becomes the tendency to relinquish literature's role as a "criticism of life" is already evident in T. S. Eliot, who in 1933 wrote, "Any theory which relates poetry very closely to a religious or a social scheme of things aims, probably, to *explain* poetry by discovering its natural laws; but it is in danger of *binding* poetry by legislation— and poetry can recognize no such laws."[3]

These writers and critics of the early twentieth century foreshadow the gradual movement toward the view that language is the defining element of literature, but all of them predate Wellek and Warren's *Theory of Literature,* the book which in the 1940s most clearly articulated the view that literature is best understood in relation to language:

The term "literature" seems best if we limit it to the art of literature, that is, to imaginative literature. . . . The simplest way of solving the question [of what counts as imaginative literature] is by distinguishing the particular use made of language in literature. Language is the material of literature as stone or bronze is that of sculpture, paints of pictures, or sounds of music. . . . The main distinctions to be drawn are between the literary, the everyday, and the scientific uses of language.[4]

While theorists since Wellek and Warren have varied in their acceptance or criticism of the effort to define literature as a special kind or use of language, most have assumed the underlying principle. The central issues of literary theory and interpretation have been questions of language. Northrop Frye's *Anatomy of Criticism* is representative:

We think . . . of literature at first as a commentary on an external "life" or "reality." But just as in mathematics we have to go from three apples to three, and from a square field to a square, so in reading a novel we have to go from literature as reflection of life to literature as autonomous language. . . . Pure literature, like pure mathematics, contains its own meaning.[5]

Differences among contemporary theorists often come to expression in conflicting theories of language, but no matter how far apart their views of language may be, they still typically assume that literary studies must be grounded in a theory of language. David Bleich, whose title *Subjective Criticism* declares his privileging of the *subject,* does not conceive of the *subject* in a Cartesian sense of an autonomous entity but in relation to the subjective origin of language: "Most fundamentally, subjective literature calls attention to the complex subjective actions of language. If we are not conscious of language use, we are not aware of how decisively it defines our realities. . . . In fact, reality is identified with linguistic reality."[6] Bleich's extreme position is quite different from John Ellis's effort to follow Wittgenstein in *The Theory of Literary Criticism: A Logical Analysis.* But Ellis, too, while scorning the question of the origin of literature and focusing on its use, also regards the central question as one of language: literature, he says, comprises "those pieces of language used in a certain way by the community."[7]

Literary theorists have concentrated for so long on the question of language that it is difficult to conceive of a theory which does not make language its central concern. Interestingly, the tone of the more recent assertions about language differs markedly from the tone of the comments of earlier critics. The difference is essentially this: whereas the earlier critics conceived of language as the means whereby literature could talk about life, the recent critics define literature as language and then ask how it is possible for language to talk about life. The earlier assumption is that literature and life are mutually illuminating, even though language as the vehicle of this illumination may be problematical. The current assumption is that language and literature are mutually illuminating, and whether literature illuminates life depends on how we conceive of language. The assumption that a literary theory depends on a theory of language rather than a theory of life is the dogmatic undercurrent of almost all discussion of textuality. Thus Paul de Man writes, "I would not hesitate to equate the rhetorical, figural potentiality of language with literature itself."[8]

It may be that the continuing debates over textual criticism will not advance until the identification of literature with language is sufficiently challenged by an alternative view. That alternative might lie in the recent discussions of action theory,[9] and perhaps a new "literature-as-action" model will in time radically shift the direction of literary and hermeneutical reflection. Literature, action theory claims, is not first of all a species of language, but is rather a species of action. Language, in this view, provides a means whereby certain actions may be performed. The main thesis is that authors use language to form texts; in so doing, they also perform related actions and make possible the performance of certain additional actions by readers.

In the remainder of this chapter I explore these two models of hermeneutics. As a critical guide to the literature-as-language model, I will focus on the work of Jacques Derrida, both because Derrida has become one of the most influential figures in contemporary hermeneutical debates[10] and because the key issues appear in such striking fashion in his work. In the subsequent five sections, I will compare the literature-as-language model to the action model and observe how the latter helps overcome the limits of the former.

The Limits of the Literature-as-Language Model

Perhaps no one has demonstrated the limits of the literature-as-language model more dramatically than Jacques Derrida, both in his critique of what he calls the logocentrism of Western thought and in his own alternative proposals. Derrida has excited both avid disciples and harsh critics, an indication of how forcefully his philosophical excavations have uncovered our buried assumptions about language. Derrida will not let old bones lie. But, once disturbed, can these bones live? Derrida says yes, and that is the stirring call which his followers hear.

> Such a flower [a heliotrope, which Derrida uses as an image for metaphorical language] always bears within itself its own double, whether it be the seed or the type, the chance of its program or the necessity of its diagram. The heliotrope may always raise itself up. And it may always become a dried flower in a book; and because of the endless repetition in which it is endlessly spoilt, no language can bring within its compass the structure of an anthology. Anthology is powerless before this supplemented code in which the field is crossed, the fences endlessly shifted, the line confused, the circle opened.
>
> Unless an anthology were also a lithography. Indeed, the heliotrope is a stone, too: a precious stone, greenish and veined with red, a kind of Eastern jasper.[11]

Derrida's penetrating look at the nature of human language reveals its encrustation by outmoded metaphysics, but it also uncovers the creative potential which still exists within the marrow of those old bones. Derrida's philosophy is a philosophy of creativity, not one of dissolution. Hermeneutics is, for him, the process whereby we encounter the ambiguity in texts and in all cultural products and find in the very ambiguity new possibilities for thought and action.

At the heart of Derrida's attempt to revivify language in an age of sterile formalism is his conception of "writing" *(écriture)*[12] as the fundamental human activity. "Writing" is not simply the inscription of thought or speech in the languages of different cultures. "Writing" precedes the inscription of thought. Derrida's point may perhaps be clarified if we contrast his metaphor of "writing" the world (as distinguished from inscribing a text) to the more familiar metaphor of "reading" the world. We commonly speak of "reading the evidence" or "reading the world" as an action prior to our writing of a text which encodes our "reading." But according to Derrida the world does not exist *for us* as a metaphysical given prior to our act of "writing" it. Rather, the world as we are able to know it comes into existence *for us* in and through our acts of "writing." The metaphor of "reading" the world would be alien to Derrida's thought because it assumes that, prior to reading, a world is already "present," waiting to be read.

The concept of "writing," thus, goes hand in hand with Derrida's rejection of traditional metaphysics. A theory of language and understanding must begin, in his view, from a radically nonmetaphysical and nonrealist starting point. Philosophies which argue that our language is grounded in a knowable reality which precedes language are philosophies of "presence," or what Derrida calls logocentric philosophies. Derrida argues, in contrast, that language cannot be grounded in metaphysical certainties and that we should speak therefore of "absence" rather than "presence." "Absence" does not imply a denial of metaphysical reality (for that in itself would be a metaphysical claim) but only that such affirmation or denial is beyond the capabilities of language. And since language defines the boundaries of theoretical thought, we can only be aware of the "absence" from our thought of that which is beyond thought.

What enables Derrida to give life to this modern rejection of metaphysics is a conception of the profound historicity of all human activity. If all cultural activity is time-bound, no human activity can transcend history. But this does not mean that action is wholly shaped or determined by already existing cultural situations. Human action is not simply contained within or determined by a culture; rather, culture arises out of and is continually reshaped by originary acts of "writing" which reveal the historical origins of culture itself.

By raising the question of the originary action which must be both historical and outside or prior to the structures of cultural experience, Derrida reinforces his claim to move beyond the traditions of Western metaphysics, which in his view are predicated on a notion of the anteriority of an object or subject in terms of which man may be conceived. For Derrida the fundamental historicity of life makes it impossible to conceive of something prior to human action *per se,* for of every action whatsoever we may ask "What is prior?" That question, of course, is unanswerable apart from *a priori* assumptions about the nature of reality. This radical indescribability of man and his culture apart from assumptions that are themselves culturally determined makes the entire metaphysical project, in Derrida's view, an impossible one. Even to imagine such a project already implies a move away from a radical conception of history in which every human action has an origin which cannot be fully described because it necessarily precedes whatever is known.

What remains to be said, therefore, is simply that culture and language are products of prior acts of "writing" *(écriture)* which are witness to the indescribable and unexplainable origin of "writing" itself as man's first step into culture and language. In Derrida's terminology this originary action of "writing" can be thought of under the related concept of the *trace.*[13] Every human act makes an observable mark on or in culture, but every cultural mark also gives evidence of its origin in some human action whose sources and operations cannot be entirely specified. The *mark* we make by our "writing" is also a *trace* of the indeterminate origin of our "writing." Because the origin of "writing" is forever prior to the point at which cultural analysis and understanding can begin, the *trace* testifies to the ultimate indescribability of the source of "writing."

It is erroneous to charge that Derrida's view is pessimistic or nihilistic because it condemns us to uncertainty about what is; rather, for Derrida, this view liberates us from untenable metaphysical theories which assume that knowledge must be grounded in metaphysical claims either about the self or the world. As the concept of the trace suggests, nothing at all can be known about the metaphysical origin of "writing," and hence the act of "writing" is not circumscribed by theories, pessimistic or not. And if, as Derrida holds, acts of "writing" form a continuous process of action and take place in all of our cultural activities, then the concepts of "writing" and the trace indicate not only the limits of thought but also the inexhaustible possibility and creativity of thought and culture. Derrida's work can be read as a rejection of cultural pessimism and an affirmation of human freedom.

The term Derrida uses for his hermeneutical method—*deconstruction*[14]—may suggest tearing down rather than building up. But, as we shall see, deconstruction is simply the consistent application of Derrida's conception of history and meaning. If every act of "writing" is historically innovative and different from every other act, and if no metaphysics of identity can obtain, there would appear to be no principle of continuity to establish relationships of meaning. If everything is indeterminate in a metaphysical sense, how can we account for continuity in a world of change? Derrida's position is Heraclitian rather than Parmenidean: if metaphysics were possible, we would need to account for change in a unified world; but since metaphysics is not possible in a world which is radically historical, we need to account for continuity in a diversified world.

For Derrida continuity is given in the cultural marks which result from and give form to our acts of "writing." Far from proposing to denigrate or "tear down" our cultural history, Derrida's theory exalts history as the only thing which we have as human beings. Historical acts can be understood only in their relationships to one another as man's attempt to "write," that is, to act meaningfully in his cultural situations. Since we never write in a historical vacuum, our acts always have a cultural specificity even though they are not wholly determined by culture. The attempt to do justice both to the inescapability of culture and the indeterminacy of meaning gives Derrida's view its peculiar forcefulness and, to his followers, its persuasiveness.

Because in every act we have both the trace of an originating moment and the mark of cultural specificity, every act of "writing" has a determinate meaning and an indeterminate meaning. The determinate meaning of our cultural acts is always made ambivalent by the *trace,* that is, the evidence of their origination in sources of action which are not culture-bound. Thus, actions shaped by a culture also function to modify that culture. In this way culture is continuously being interpreted, changed, and undermined even while it exerts its formative influences on our living and thinking. The continuity of culture is being continuously challenged by the very acts which give it continuity. Thus, every hermeneutical analysis which attempts to understand an action or a text by showing its place in the continuity of actual historical culture must also show its discontinuity with that same culture. This, then, is the deconstructive method. In practice the deconstructionists may emphasize the hidden signs of discontinuity which are in every text more than the apparent signs of continuity (more traditional approaches stress the constructive side), but the deconstructive method is not in spirit negative or culture-denying. What it affirms is human freedom and creativity.

With this in mind we can see the import of Derrida's key term *differance,*[15] a word which combines as equal and inseparable elements in every act of "writing" the feature of *differing* and the feature of *deferring.* When we examine written texts (or any other cultural acts), we see that their constructive meaning emerges in their differences from other texts, but we also note that by virtue of the trace their meaning cannot be fully determinate, and thus they in some way make provisional the very meaning they intend to construct. While their determinate meaning establishes their continuity with other acts and texts in a given cultural situation through the quality of *difference,* the indeterminate meaning creates change and thus their meaning is also *deferred.* Meaning thus is *differance*—an inseparable union of the concepts to *differ* and to *defer*—and hermeneutics is the process through which we attempt to deal with the inevitable ambiguity in the interpretive process. Because this process is never completed, meaning is forever indeterminate and changing. Every reader interprets texts in relation to his own cultural situation and thereby participates in the endless, ever-changing process of exploring and creating meaning. Interpretation itself is always a new act of "writing" and participates in the creative and free interplay of human culture.

What does this summary of Derrida's position reveal about the "literature-as-language" model? First, it implies a skeptical view of the relation between words and things while at the same time seizing upon the positive consequences of this skepticism. While, for Derrida, words cannot be said to refer to metaphysical realities, the loss of the metaphysical connection makes possible a historical understanding of reference. Words refer not to things as metaphysical substances or "things in themselves," but to things as they appear to us in our acts of "writing," to things as we form them for ourselves through language. While the language model closes for us the metaphysical quest for a determinate logocentric understanding of things, it at the same time opens for us the endless exploration of a world of things in their historical concreteness and immediacy. Our lives, thus, can be seen as a continuous play made possible by the indeterminate or ambivalent relationship of words and things.

Second, Derrida's analysis disallows any conception of *mimesis* which holds that words give us a true picture of reality. Even if words refer to things formed by our "writing," they cannot "picture life" for us as it "really" is, for the trace and mystery of origins make the referential force of language ambivalent and self-erasing. On Derrida's view, no statements can be taken as truthful in an absolute sense, though that is not to say that they are false either. Concepts of absolute truth and falsity as traditionally formulated reflect the kind of metaphysical thinking that Derrida believes he has refuted. Any conception of *mimesis* which barters in the coinage of absolute truth and falsity must be abandoned, for whether the world that we "write" and constantly "rewrite" is ultimately true or false can never be known.

Thus, third, Derrida's critique reveals the radical relativism implicit in theories which hold that meaning can be determined by the interior rationality of language and that truth can be discovered in and through language *per se*. Derrida's position is that the conflicting claims of relativist and nonrelativist theories are subject to the same deconstructive analysis: in the very conflicts raised by their respective claims they reveal that language is created by us as our means for leaving our marks on a world we are continuously forming by our "writing." Language, thus, is not autonomous but historical, not the originary source and center of meaning but one of the products—revealing both mark and trace—of "writing." Derrida's skepticism about truth and language is not for him a debilitating view; indeed, it unlocks and glorifies human creativity. Yet in his view the "deconstruction" of logocentric theories of language does undermine the epistemological foundations needed for traditional theories of meaning, truth, and reference. Such is the conclusion, too, of Richard Rorty, who examines the question from somewhat different angles.[16] The historicity of "writing" places all logocentric theories of language under a historical conditionality, and the quest for meaning and truth can be understood only as the desire to "continue the conversation" (Rorty's term) in spite of the impossibility of discovering final truth.

Before turning to the action model for hermeneutical theory, we should note the way one literary theorist has attempted to deal with the questions of truth and relativism which Derrida has raised. Paul de Man shifts the focus of hermeneutical discussion from questions of reference and mimesis to questions of rhetoric. We have rhetorical use of language, de Man reasons, when the referential power of language is suspended or indeterminate:

> The grammatical model of the questions becomes rhetorical not when we have, on the one hand, a literal meaning and on the other hand a figural meaning, but when it is impossible to decide by grammatical or other linguistic devices which of the two meanings (that can be entirely incompatible) prevails. Rhetoric radically suspends logic and opens up vertiginous possibilities of referential aberration.[17]

Rhetoric, as the deployment of language where reference cannot be finally determined, characterizes "literature itself." Is it possible, de Man asks, for hermeneutics really to "unite outer meaning with inner understanding, action with reflection, into one single totality?"[18] De Man attempts to show that a literary text "simultaneously asserts and denies the authority of its own rhetorical mode."[19] Rhetorical ambivalence marks all literature, and the analysis of rhetorical ambivalence will be "the task of literary criticism in the coming years."[20] As a consequence, questions of reference appear unimportant for literary hermeneutics; literature exists precisely where the question of reference does not occur. Literature presents to us a rhetoric in which textual meaning is ambivalent and in which extratextual reference cannot resolve the ambivalence. In short, de Man seems to say, the problems of literature are not the problems of language generally, for literature is a subcategory in which we find a certain rhetorical use of language. The ambivalence of literature creates in us an "anxiety (or bliss . . .) of ignorance, not an anxiety of reference."[21]

Thus, while de Man works within the same philosophical framework as Derrida, he bypasses the issues of truth and reference by viewing literature as a special rhetorical use of language. The result is that de Man offers a theory of the autonomy of the literary text which in certain ways is more sophisticated than formalist and structuralist theories but which, like them, tries to distinguish literary texts from nonliterary texts on the basis of language functions. De Man readily acknowledges that the "notion of a language entirely freed of referential constraints is properly inconceivable," but he finds in literature a reversal of "the traditional priority" of a referential meaning over the internal meaning of the language of the text. This reversal of the traditional priorities "asserts itself in Rilke's poetry by disguising itself at once into its opposite,"[22] but although the language of Rilke's poems appears to be referential, it is clear, de Man argues, that "the *priority of lexis* over *logos* is always apparent" in the *structure* of his poems. Deconstruction of the dynamics of literary rhetoric is thus the goal of hermeneutics, and for this the philosophical problems of reference may be set aside.

But de Man's project is not as innocent as it might appear, because for him literature is not really just one of the ways in which language works—it is the paradigmatic way. Consider the following:

> The first step of the Nietzschean deconstruction therefore reminds us, as in the above quotation, of the figurality of all language.
>
> To the extent that all language is conceptual, it always already speaks about language and not about things. . . . All language is language about denomination, that is, a conceptual, figural metaphorical metalanguage. . . . If all language is about language, then the paradigmatic-linguistic model is that of an entity that confronts itself.
>
> Language can only be about something such as man (i.e., conceptual), but in being about man, it can never know whether it is about anything at all including itself, since it is precisely the *aboutness,* the referentiality, that is in question.[23]

Referentiality is a necessary concept, de Man agrees, but "since the convergence of the referential and the figural signification can never be established, the reference can never be a meaning."[24] By the end of his book *Allegories of Reading* de Man is speaking not just of literary texts as a special category but of all texts, of which literature is the privileged model: "There can be no use of language which is not, within a certain perspective, thus radically formal, i.e., mechanical, no matter how deeply this aspect may be cancelled by aesthetic, formalistic, delusions."[25] Though he is analyzing Rousseau here, the message is de Man's as well as Rousseau's. In the final analysis, de Man's camel of literary rhetoric takes over the whole tent of language, and his own rhetoric resembles Derrida's hermeneutics of suspicion: "In conformity with a paradox that is inherent in all literature, the poetry [of Rilke] gains a maximum of convincing power at the very moment that it abdicates any claim to truth."[26] In de Man as in Derrida the literature-as-language model ends in a radically skeptical or agnostic view of reference. Derrida's call to "play" is somewhat different in tone from de Man's call to "ironize," but both proceed from a similar rigor in the unmasking of language.

Basic Principles of the Literature-as-Action Model

Although the action model we will explore in the following sections reclaims the importance of reference and the nonlinguistic world, it recognizes the value of Derrida's stress on the historicality of all our cultural acts. It also derives support from the increasing awareness in recent hermeneutical discussions—as, for example, in Hans-Georg Gadamer and Paul Ricoeur—of the historical contexts of both texts and interpretations.

Synchronic ahistorical models for the structural analysis of texts and other cultural phenomena fail to account for a text's relationship to extratextual situations which precede and follow it. Ferdinand de Saussure, whose linguistic theories have been the source for many structuralist models, was himself well aware of the limits of synchronic analysis. Indeed, he devoted as much space in his *Course in General Linguistics* to diachronic linguistics as he did to synchronic linguistics.[27] For him, however, diachronic linguistics is still a formalized linguistics, concerned only with changes over time in the structural relationships of signifier (sound-image) to signified (concept). Sound-images become associated with concepts in new and changing ways over time, but these changes are purely formal and may be described linguistically apart from general theories of reference, meaning, and truth, that is, apart from historical interpretations which go beyond linguistics. The interpretation of linguistic change, in short, is not equivalent to an interpretation of history.

Formal theories of texts, too, examine the diachronic as well as the synchronic character of texts within a formalized system, but they cannot yield an adequate view of the relation of texts to that which is nontextual or nonformal. The description of any formalized system—whether diachronic or synchronic—can never account in a *comprehensive* way for the historical conditions of its own existence. Thus, by raising in a radical way the question of origins Derrida has sharply focused the dilemma of purely formalized theories and exposed the fundamental inescapability of the historicity of thought. For every formalizable system there is a prior originary moment. Focusing on language and other sign systems, structuralist and semiotic models regard language as a self-contained system whose manifestations are to be understood primarily through structural analysis. But in the aftermath of poststructuralist critiques of language,[28] theories which concentrate on the structural and formal properties of texts have become increasingly inadequate. Because language is not a semiotic system which absorbs and contains history but one which emerges from history, theories of linguistic autonomy seem headed for the same impasse as theories which have posited the autonomy of reason.

In this situation action theory offers a new approach to the understanding of language by claiming that action is a larger and more basic category than language. Language is not prior to or more primary than action, but it is a product of human action and also a means whereby we perform certain kinds of action. Language is never autonomous and context-free. It is a means, an instrument, an enabling device for some of the actions of human beings. If everything that human beings do or can do (other than natural or involuntary happenings) is an instance of action, then both the development and use of language are actions, and the writing and reading of texts are actions. An action model of hermeneutics, thus, tries to show how language and texts function in the context of all human actions.

In developing an action model of hermeneutics, we will be chiefly concerned with texts as instances of inscribed language, as the products of the action of inscribing. Action, of course, is not a unique property of such texts, for the writing and interpreting of texts are but two examples of innumerable kinds of human actions. The writing and interpreting of texts are, however, actions which occasion and make possible the performance of other actions. This observation is clarified by Nicholas Wolterstorff, who in his aesthetics makes a distinction between texts as objects and texts as instruments,[29] two aspects of texts which we will consider in succession.

We perform many actions with the goal of producing objects, and among these objects are written texts. The existence of these texts is not an autonomous existence, for they are products of action and must be understood as elements in a structure of action. The language of the text, too, cannot be understood as having a meaning in a self-contained sense but only by virtue of its existence as a part of action. Any language theory adequate for hermeneutics must be set within a theory of action. Because texts are objects produced by actions, one can speak "objectively" about a text only in the framework of the actions that have produced the text. To understand a text objectively is not to deploy an incorrigible method of disinterested analysis but to understand the text as an object produced by certain actions.

But texts are not only objects of action; they are also instruments of action. We may perform certain actions—such as communicating with others, describing nature, expressing emotion, articulating philosophical theories, and praising God—by means of texts. Hermeneutics, thus, must not conceive of texts simply as objects which have certain properties but also as instruments which we use to perform various kinds of actions. In this approach to hermeneutics we no longer have any reason to regard the meaning of a text as something wholly contained within the language of the text. Rather, we must explore what it means to say that the language of the text is an instrument as well as an object of action.

A second general principle is that the meaning or "sense" of a sentence or text depends not only upon internal structure but also upon the situation in which sentences occur and the purposes for which they are used. The word *meaning* causes many difficulties in literary discussions because it almost universally connotes the idea of a self-contained "sense" lodged within the sentences of a text. For this reason we should perhaps say that an action theory of texts concentrates on *function* rather than *meaning*. The proper question for hermeneutics is "What actions are being performed by the making and use of this text?" Meaning is contingent upon actions and is not autonomously contained in the language of texts.

To clarify this general statement, let us examine the relation of the linguistic structure of a sentence to its semantic function. Every sentence has a subject which identifies what the subject stands for and a predicate which indicates what is being predicated about the subject. But in addition the sentence as a whole may be used to say something, that is, to form a proposition. To illustrate, let us take the sentence "David will go tomorrow." We may use this sentence to *identify* a person David about which we *predicate* something, namely that he will go tomorrow. But in addition we may use the sentence as a whole to say that David will go tomorrow. These three things—identifying, predicating, saying—are distinguishable. We use the predicate to say of David that he will go tomorrow, but we could use these words to predicate the same thing of Joe or Bill or anyone. Similarly we use the subject to identify David, but we could use that same subject to identify any number of persons or things named "David." What we do by way of the sentence as a whole, however, is to say that David will go tomorrow. We use the combination of subject and predicate to perform an action (saying) which is distinguishable from the actions of identifying and predicating.

The need for these distinctions is evident in two ways. First, many sentences include what philosophers of language call *index-*

icals, elements such as demonstrative pronouns, first-person pronouns, proper names, certain adverbs, and time indicators.[30] The reference of these indexicals can be understood only if we know the context of use; they cannot be understood from the subject and predicate alone. For example, if someone utters the sentence "David Jones will go tomorrow," we know that he is predicating of someone identified as David Jones that he will go tomorrow. But if we are to understand what he is saying by way of the sentence, we will have to know who *David Jones* is and the specific time designated by the word *tomorrow.* And these things we cannot learn from the subject and predicate alone or from the syntactic relationship of the subject and predicate. We cannot understand the "meaning" of the sentence unless we know its function in the specific situation of the sentence utterance. Indexicals are important elements in the "sense" or meaning of many sentences, but their meaning or semantic function cannot be fully discerned from the words and syntax of the sentences themselves.

Furthermore, the "sense" of a sentence depends also on what speech-action theorists call the illocutionary force of the sentence, that is, the purpose for which the sentence is used. Sentences may be used not only to assert but also to ask, command, promise, insist, concede, and the like. For example, the sentence we have been using—"David Jones will go tomorrow"—could be used to insist, concede, or promise as well as to assert. But its use in any particular situation can be known only if we know the context of its use. The illocutionary force of a sentence cannot be determined from the language or syntax alone. Thus, because of the presence of indexicals we will in many instances have to look beyond the sentence in order to understand what is being said by the sentence; and always we will have to go beyond the sentence in order to determine the illocutionary force of its utterance.

A third general principle that is relevant for an action theory of hermeneutics has to do with the temporal nature of actions. They begin at a given moment, move through subsequent moments, and come to an end. The objects that are produced by our actions cannot be fully understood apart from the sequence of actions which produces them; they are not autonomous or self-contained in their meaning.[31] The import of this principle can be seen clearly when we move from the sentences of the text to the text as a whole.

Roman Ingarden offers one of the most rigorous attempts to define a text as an object possessing self-contained meaning. In his book *The Literary Work of Art*[32] he argues that although texts are not ontically autonomous, as are objects in nature, they also are not psychically contingent, that is, they are not objects which exist only in the minds of authors and readers. A text is an object whose meaning is given in the "many-layered structure" of which the text as an intentional object is composed. Ingarden argues that the language of the text projects "purely intentional correlates" as the objects to which the words and sentences refer. In the case of real judgments or scientific descriptions the intentional correlates are the truly existing objects that we encounter in actual experience; however, in the case of literary or fictional judgments and descriptions, the intentional correlates only simulate real objects; they are "quasi-objects," *analogues* of real objects and states of affairs. A literary text as a whole, then, projects an imagined world made up of imagined objects and states of affairs. A literary text exists as a purely intentional object whose intentioned world is imagined rather than real.

Ingarden's theory proposes that the meanings of sentences are "intended" or given in the language of the sentences and that the words of sentences point beyond themselves to intentional objects. It seems evident, however, that words and sentences do not of themselves have intentions or intentional correlates but have them only as a consequence of the speech-actions of those who utter the words and sentences. Because of the ways we use our language, we do correlate words and things such that the words themselves appear to hold or "intend" certain meanings: the word *apple,* for example, refers to a certain kind of fruit, not just to any kind. But words acquire dependable or "intended" meanings only because we habitually associate them with certain objects and use them for certain purposes. The meanings are not lodged in the words *per se* but in our continued use of the words for certain purposes and in certain ways.

In support of his view Ingarden argues that the intentional meanings of a literary text are established for us by the interrelationships of language structures through the entire text. These linguistic interdependencies create in the text various "strata" or structures of meaning which fix the meanings which the author intends. The result is that in very complex ways the language-structures contain an "intentional" meaning apart from the author. An analysis of the "many-layered" strata of a text will, in Ingarden's view, discover the intended meaning of the text. Such a position seems also to be implied in Paul Ricoeur's view of the intentionality of the text. A written text, Ricoeur says, exists at some distance from its author and hence must be interpreted as a language-structure independent of its author; since the author is no longer present to be questioned, the meanings must be derived from the language of the text.[33] For Ricoeur, as for Ingarden, this is not a disastrous situation, for the text has certain structures which contain the "sense" of the text. By analyzing the structure of the text we may discover its intentionality, that is, the world which it intends to disclose.

Although Ingarden and Ricoeur argue that the intentional meanings of a text can be derived from the structural relationships established by the text's language, many texts contain words whose intentional correlates we cannot understand simply in terms of intratextual relationships. For example, in "On First Looking into Chapman's Homer" Keats writes:

> Much have I travell'd in the realms of gold,
>   and many goodly states and kingdoms seen;
>   Round many western islands have I been
> Which bards in fealty to Apollo hold.
> Oft of one wide expanse had I been told
>   That deep brow'd Homer ruled as his demesne . . .

Every gloss on this poem takes the word *Homer* in line six as a reference to the Homer who stands behind *The Iliad* and *The Odyssey*. Yet on Ingarden's view this could not be the case. At best the Homer of line six could only be an analogue of the actual Homer, since a literary text refers only to intentional or "quasi" objects, not to actual objects. The view that the literary Homer is an analogue of the historical Homer requires a theory of the relationship between historical realities and the intentional analogues of literary texts. Without one we have no right to use historical information as a gloss. Furthermore, if the intentional correlate of the word *Homer* exists as a quasi object distinct from the real "object" that is the Greek poet Homer, then every literary text which uses the word *Homer* must project a distinct quasi object. In that case there is potentially (in literary texts) an infinite number of intentional correlates for the word *Homer,* each one of which is distinct from all the others and none of which is identical with the Greek poet named Homer. Even if such a conception were possible, the relationships among those distinct correlates and among the recurrences of the word *Homer* would remain problematical. It appears more intuitively correct to hold that all uses of the word *Homer* (when designating the Greek poet) have as their correlate the Homer that stands behind *The Iliad*. But in that case, the correlate of the sixth line of Keats's poem is not contained exclusively in the "intentional" world of the text but appears in the actual world which exists outside the text. In more ordinary terms, the word *Homer* in line six of Keats's poem refers to the Greek poet Homer. If this is the case, we may identify certain of the referents of a literary text with the real objects of history. In those cases the "intentional correlates" of a literary text are actual objects in the real world, and their existence and meanings are not wholly contained in or explained by the language-structures of the text.

Ingarden's view that the words and sentences of a text gain their meaning from their internal structure has a certain attractiveness, but its weakness is evident even more clearly when we consider the role of authorship in textual interpretation. Theories of textual autonomy typically subordinate the importance of authorial intention and frequently ignore the signficance of authorship altogether. Ingarden deals with the question of authorial intention by treating it as a problem of narrative voice. He distinguishes several kinds of narrative strategies, but for him the narrator is always thought to be within the world of the text; what he calls the "center of orientation" is "always to be found within the represented world. . . ."[34] Even when the narrator is not a character in the narrative, Ingarden holds that

> if the narrator does not expressly belong to the represented world, the orientational space may be chosen in such a way that it is indeed found in the represented world but at the same time is not localized in any of the represented objects. . . . It is as if an invisible and never determinately represented person were wandering through the represented world and showing us the objects as they appear from his point of view. In this manner the narrator is nevertheless corepresented.[35]

This view has become the reigning view in formalist literary criticism and is frequently marked by a sharp distinction between the real historical author and an "implied author" who is identified by the narrative voice evident in the text. In its simple form it was summed up by Walker Gibson thirty years ago:

> It is now common in the classroom as well as in criticism to distinguish carefully between the author of a literary work of art and the fictitious *speaker* within the work of art. . . . It is this speaker who is real in the sense most useful to the study of literature, for the speaker is made of language alone, and his entire self lies on the page before us in evidence.[36]

If we wish to defend textual autonomy, we will need to ignore authorial intention and posit the presence of an "implied author" who is distinct from the real author of a text. But if texts do not autonomously contain all the data needed for interpretation, then the narrative voice of the text may be considered in relation to the real author whose actions in forming the text are relevant to textual understanding.

Thus in action theory the issue of authorship once again assumes importance, and new ways of dealing with it become possible. A text may or may not express the intentions an author had in mind while inscribing the text, but even if it does not, the text's failure to do so does not make irrelevant the actions of the author. We distinguish between what the author intends to do and what the author actually does. The two may coincide (and perhaps usually do), but they do not necessarily coincide. In textual studies, many, following Ingarden, take this distinction as equivalent to the distinction between the author's subjective intentions and the text's intentionality, and then, putting aside a psychologistic concern with the author's states of mind, focus on the intentionality which the text itself presumably displays. Thus, in common practice, authorship becomes effectually irrelevant.

In an action theory, knowledge about the author's intentions is not *necessary* for interpretation, but an awareness of the author's actions in forming a text makes us more conscious of the author's presence in a text and more willing to recognize the potential value of a knowledge of those intentions. Even aside from intentions, however, what an author *does* in forming a text is always crucial to hermeneutics, and we can analyze these actions apart from what the author subjectively intended. In that analysis, we can examine the ways in which an author uses language and the ways in which the author's actions enable language to function. We do this by setting texts in the context of history and by showing their role as objects and instruments in a temporal process of interrelated actions.

In the following sections we will investigate how texts are tied to the actions of authors and readers. Like Ingarden we will examine how the meanings of texts are related to their structures and language, but unlike Ingarden we have no epistemological reason to develop a strategy which effaces the author, supplanting him with a concept of textual intentionality. We therefore abandon the notion of textual intentionality and focus rather on how textual structures arise out of the actions of authors.

The Questions of Reference and Mimesis

The foregoing discussion provides a basis for an examination of the terms *reference* and *mimesis,* which open up for us crucial questions about how texts are related to the actions of authors and readers and how they are related to the world outside the text. In order to delineate these relationships, we will focus our attention on fictional narratives, since they present us with the most problematic cases.

Since Plato and Aristotle established *mimesis* (imitation) as a key critical concept, the term has proved to be one of the most elusive and difficult in the history of literary criticism as well as one of the most vehemently embraced and maligned notions. The reasons for this are understandable, for the relationship of texts to the world, of language to reality, is a central philosophical problem, and methods of defining that relationship are as varied as philosophy itself. In the twentieth century, the term *mimesis* has generally been suspect because of a pervasive philosophical skepticism. If reality as it is in itself is unknowable, how can we say that texts imitate reality? *Mimesis* under such conditions seems to have outlived its usefulness. In modern discussions of literary criticism the term *reference* tends to replace the term *mimesis,* and theoretical debates focus on the problem of the referentiality of language. Thus, in order to reevaluate the concept of *mimesis* we need first to examine the primary uses of the term *reference.*

We may begin by distinguishing between *concrete* and *ideal* reference. The term *concrete reference* will be used to indicate a relation of language to actual objects in the empirical world, whereas the term *ideal reference* will indicate a relation of language to the nonempirical referents of such words as *law, anger, triangle,* and the like. Ideal referents in turn may be conceived as *real* entities (as defined, for example, by Plato) or *conceptual* entities (as defined, for example, by Kant). Using these definitions we may say that most of the words constituting fictional texts do not have concrete reference, since most of the objects in a fictional narrative do not exist as objects in the empirical world: the snake that bit Jim in *Huckleberry Finn* was not an actual snake in the actual world. On the other hand, one would have to hold to an idealist metaphysics to associate the snake in *Huck Finn* with an ideal referent. One could, alternatively, suggest that fictional language refers to *concepts* that exist in the minds of authors and readers. But the notion that the referents of fictional language are conceptual entities commits one to a psychological theory of reference and all the epistemological problems which that entails.[37]

To avoid these problems, some have suggested a fourth conception of reference, namely the notion of *self-reference.* On this view the referent is available in language itself: words have meaning because their referential power is contained within them or in their relationships to other words within a language system. We should not search for the referent for the snake that bit Jim in the actual world (concrete reference) or in an ideal world (ideal reference) or in the minds of readers (conceptual reference) but in the words themselves (self-reference). This view has been expressed by some structuralists; Tzvetan Todorov, for example, says:

> Literature enjoys, therefore, a particularly privileged status among semiotic activities. It has language as both its point of departure and its destination; language furnishes literature as its abstract configurations as well as its perceptible material— it is both mediator and mediatized.[38]

This self-referential view of language should not be associated with Saussure, as it sometimes erroneously is. Nor should it be taken as a psychological theory of reference, since the referents are understood to be contained within language itself and not simply in the minds of readers.

Some literary theorists have adopted an alternative strategy for dealing with problems of referentiality by claiming that fictional language is nonreferential. They argue that if reference designates the relationship of words to things, then fictional language is different from ordinary language because fictional language has no referents that actually exist. This view may be seen in John Ellis's *The Theory of Literary Criticism: A Logical Analysis:*

> Nowhere in current theory of literature is it clearer than in the dispute over the problem of definition [of literature] that the reference theory of meaning is the barrier to progress. . . .
>
> Of these [commonsense notions of the logic of language], the most pervasive, and therefore the most pernicious for literary theory, has been the reference theory of meaning.[39]

A variant of this view is evident in the position taken by Michael Riffaterre, who suggests that in literary texts the referential aspect of language must be transcended:

> This is proof at least [the point here concerns a critic who was too preoccupied with literal or referential meaning] that no matter what the poem ultimately tells us that may be quite different from ordinary ideas about the real, the message has been so constructed that the reader has to leap the hurdle of reality.
>
> Thus, what makes the poem, what constitutes its message, has little to do with what it tells us or with the language it employs. It has everything to do with the way the given twists the mimetic codes out of shape by substituting its own structure for their structures.[40]

The denial of referentiality stems from the desire to avoid the philosophical positions on which theories of reference seem to depend. A more general stategy for dealing with referentiality is possible, however. By introducing a conception of *descriptive reference* we may place certain philosophical problems at one remove from the problems of textual interpretation. By using the term *descriptive reference* we claim that language is inconceivable without a notion of reference, but we are not committed to a particular theory about the ontological status of those objects that are descriptively pointed out. All language refers to objects and states of affairs in a descriptive way, that is, it refers to them simply by pointing them out. In the case of fiction the words *Huck Finn* refer to the person Huckleberry Finn descriptively. The issues surrounding the ontological status of Huck Finn as a fictional character may be held in abeyance. In short, all language has descriptive reference, however one defines the nature of the referent.

With these distinctions in hand, let us propose a way of seeing the relationship between *reference* and *mimesis*. The language of a novel descriptively refers to the fictional objects and states of affairs that the author picks out or projects by means of the language. We may regard these objects and states of affairs as constituting the world of the novel. As long as we limit our concern to the descriptive references of the novel's language, we are only surveying or mapping out its fictional world, that is, seeing clearly the states of affairs that are being pointed out. For example, the language of *Huckleberry Finn* refers descriptively to the states of affairs in which Huck Finn finds himself in Mark Twain's novel. Our concern with reference is a concern only with an accurate understanding of what these states of affairs are. After the world that Huck Finn inhabits has been surveyed, however, other interesting and difficult questions arise concerning the significance of the novel, its aesthetic merits, its social and moral value for us as readers, its relationship to its contemporary historical setting, and the like. These subsequent questions involve the ways in which the fictional world of the text is related to the actual world of the readers, and these are questions of mimesis. We are proposing, then, that the term *reference* be used to indicate the relationship of the language of the text to the world that is projected by the language, and that the word *mimesis* be used to indicate the relationship of the fictional world projected by the text to the actual world that we inhabit.

The failure to distinguish clearly between reference and mimesis lies behind certain problems in contemporary literary theory, problems which are exemplified in Wolfgang Iser's recent and important book *The Act of Reading*.[41] Iser repeatedly calls attention to the fact that fictional texts cannot refer to real things: "However, it must be borne in mind that fictional texts constitute their own objects and do not copy something already in existence." This observation leads Iser to conclude: "For this reason they cannot have the total determinacy of real objects, and, indeed, it is the elements of indeterminacy that enable the text to 'communicate' with the reader, in the sense that they induce him to participate both in the production and comprehension of the work's intention."[42] Because it lacks concrete reference, Iser says, the literary text is like an iconic sign which designates "the condition of *con*ception and *per*ception which enables the observer to construct the object intended by the signs." Here the signs of the fictional text appear not to refer to anything given in the text ("for there is no given object except for the sign itself"[43]), and the referents apparently must be constructed in the minds of readers according to the directions given by the signs.

Yet at other points Iser seems equally wary of a subjective and psychological view of reference and speaks of the text as representing to the reader not just signs or a set of directives but also a "world" that is given in and through the language:

> We may assume that every literary text in one way or another represents a perspective view of the world put together by (though not necessarily typical of) the author. As such, the work is in no way a mere copy of the given world—it constructs a world of its own out of the material available to it. It is the way in which this world is constructed that brings about the perspective of the author.[44]

Iser clearly, however, does not think the world constructed by the text consists of the determinate states of affairs projected by the language and constituting its referents. Precisely this *lack* of determinate reference leads Iser to believe that the work exists in the interaction between the language of the text and the consciousness of the reader. In the process of reading, the reader actualizes the potential meanings of the linguistic signs: "Text and reader converge by way of a situation which depends on both for its 'realization.' "[45]

When Iser uses the term *reality,* he does not mean to indicate concrete references or state of affairs projected by a text but to designate the text's worldview or a structural model of the world:

> The term *reality* is already suspect in this connection, for no literary text relates to contingent reality as such, but to models or concepts of reality, in which contingencies and complexities are reduced to a meaningful structure. We call these structures world-pictures or systems.[46]

Iser wants to deny the referential function of fictional language while retaining the notion that fiction provides in its structural patterns "the thought systems which it has chosen and incorporated in its own repertoire."[47] The power of a novel to present "thought systems or models of reality" apparently comes from the fact that in fictional language reference is suspended:

> Denotation presupposes some form of reference that will indicate the specific meaning of the thing denoted. The literary text, however, takes its selected objects out of their pragmatic context and so shatters their original frame of reference; the result is to reveal aspects (e.g., of social norms) which had remained hidden as long as the frame of reference remained intact.[48]

Thus, while the text presents no "reality" in the sense of concrete reference, it does offer us a view or model of reality.

Using the terminology we have suggested above, we can say that Iser denies a referential function to fictional texts but retains their mimetic function. But can this be done? The problems are numerous. First, if we conceive of texts as sign systems which guide the actualizing of the fictional world in the minds of readers, is not the world which is actualized the one *referred* to by the language of the text, and is not Iser implicitly presenting a conceptual theory of reference even though he appears to deny that fictional language has reference? Second, is it possible to speak of "models of reality" given in fiction on the view that fictional words are only directional signs? It is difficult to see how the text as a set of directional signs could represent a "model of reality" or "thought-system" or "world picture" without the intervening step of the conceptual correlates associated with directional signs. It would appear that Iser's "models of reality" would have to be based on the conceptual correlates or referents of directional signs rather than on the signs conceived simply as a set of nonconceptual linguistic iconic marks.

These difficulties can perhaps best be observed in a passage where Iser discusses a particular work of fiction, Fielding's *Tom Jones*. As an illustration of how the "iconic signs of literature . . . designate *instructions* for the *production* of the signified," Iser writes:

> As an illustration, we may take the character of Allworthy in Fielding's *Tom Jones*. Allworthy is introduced to us as the perfect man, but he is at once brought face to face with a hypocrite, Captain Blifil, and is completely taken in by the latter's feigned piety. Clearly, then, the signifiers are not meant

solely to designate perfection. On the contrary, they denote instructions to the reader to build up the signified, which represents not a quality of perfection, but in fact a vital defect, namely, Allworthy's lack of judgment. The signifiers therefore do not add up to the perfection they seem to denote, but rather designate the conditions whereby perfection is to be conceived—a characteristic mode of iconic sign usage. The iconic signs fulfill their function to the degree in which their relatedness to identifiable objects begins to fade or is even blotted out. For now something has to be imagined which the signs have not denoted—though it will be preconditioned by that which they do denote. Thus the reader is compelled to transform a denotation into a connotation. In our present example, the consequence is that the "perfect man's" lack of judgment causes the reader to redefine what he means by perfection, for the signified which he has built up in turn becomes a signifier: it invokes his own concepts of perfection by means of this significant qualification (the "perfect man's" lack of judgment), not only bringing them into the conscious mind but also demanding some form of correction. Through such transformations, guided by the signs of the text, the reader is induced to construct the imaginary object. It follows that the involvement of the reader is essential to the fulfillment of the text, for materially speaking this exists only as a potential reality—it requires a "subject" (i.e., a reader) for the potential to be actualized. The literary text, then, exists primarily as a means of communication, while the process of reading is basically a kind of dyadic interaction.[49]

Iser seems to hold the view that the signifiers in *Tom Jones* could designate a quality of perfection or of a lack of judgment. But how could this be? The signifiers, it would seem, designate the characters of Allworthy and Captain Blifil and the situations in which they act, not the quality of perfection. And the presence or lack of perfection is surely represented by the characters and their actions, not directly by the signifiers. In short Iser attempts to move directly from linguistic signifiers to the "world-pictures" or worldviews which the author represents in the text. Fiction, he seems to say, leads us to adopt a way of looking at the world but does so by bypassing problems of reference.

Such a view of textual meaning seems confusing. The language of fiction does not usually have reference to states of affairs that occur in the actual world, but this does not entail the conclusion that "what is represented must be language itself."[50] All language has reference, though in the case of fiction the language refers descriptively to fictional states of affairs, not to ones in the actual world.[51] In a novel the language of the text refers to the fictionally projected states of affairs which constitute the fictional world of the novel. Because this is the case, the world of the text is designated by the language of the text and does not depend on the interaction of text and reader. In reading the novel the reader does not bring the world of the text *into existence;* rather the reader encounters it or witnesses it via the text's language. This is made possible by the text's descriptive references.

What Iser means by the text's presentation of "models of reality" is what we want to include in our concept of mimesis. Iser repeatedly argues that "models of reality" do not copy real situations and events but are possible "systems" or models for conceiving of reality. In making this claim he seems to imply that mimesis is a process of copying reality. Historically, however, mimesis has not implied that the world of the text is a realistic copy of actual states of affairs; it has implied, rather, that fictional states of affairs exhibit structural patterns of action which stand in a relation of resemblance (similarity or difference) to structural patterns of action which exist outside the text. When Aristotle described literature (art) as an imitation of an action, he was not implying a relationship between language and actual states of affairs. Instead, he held that the particular events depicted by the language of a text exhibit a structural pattern which in turn exemplifies an ideal or universal pattern of action. The language of *Oedipus Rex,* for example, gives us the story of Oedipus; the story of Oedipus exhibits a particular pattern of tragic action which we can identify and understand because of its relationship to the universal paradigmatic pattern of tragic action. Mimesis then represents the relationship of the action depicted in *Oedipus Rex* to the pattern of tragic action which can be defined extratextually as a "model" or "system." In our terminology, the language of the text is used to project an imagined world. This imagined world stands in a certain relationship—a mimetic relationship—to the actual world outside or behind the text.

Our view of mimesis, however, does not entail Aristotle's metaphysics. The patterns of action which the text "imitates" need not be conceived as universal or ideal paradigms. The patterns of action to which fictional texts stand in mimetic relationship are simply ones that the author perceives in the world as he or she experiences it and reflects on it. The mimetic relationship accounts for the historical variety and flexibility which we discover in the fictional worlds that endlessly fascinate us. But the mimetic relationship also forbids us to conceive of texts as linguistic objects cut loose from their moorings in an actual world and allowed to drift in some detached sea of aesthetic autonomy. The fictional text is not a copy of the world, but it is anchored in the world: literature is always *in* the world though it is not entirely *of* the world. To show how mimesis results from the necessary anchoring of fiction in the actual world is one of the tasks of the next section.

Imagined and Actual Worlds

We suggested in the previous section that a mimetic relationship of a fictional world to the actual world is a relation of resemblance, one of similarities and differences. Our understanding of this relationship may be clarified by the thesis that all knowledge is grounded in the comparisons we make among the states of affairs which we encounter or observe. We interpret new experiences and events in relationship to those which are already familiar to us. Objects, persons, words, or situations remain strange to us until we can place them in a frame of reference already familiar, and our understanding of new or strange phenomena depends on our ability to absorb them into familiar contexts.

We might better understand the mimetic function of imagined worlds by considering first an example of how we arrive at understanding in the case of ordinary or nonmimetic relationships. Consider the problem of understanding personal identity. How are we able to recognize a person at successive moments in time, and, indeed, over long periods of time? We recognize a person whom we have not seen for twenty years as the identical person we knew twenty years earlier in spite of the many changes that have occurred. To conceive of identity as an unchanging "essence" presents us with difficulties, for every moment alters, however slightly, the elements that constitute a person. And the conception of identity as the "essential" properties of a person still does not explain how we recognize changes in a person over time. The physical appearance of a person, of course, helps us recognize that person, but our sense of a person's identity is only partly based on physical appearance. Certainly our sense of someone's "personhood" or "personality" is not simply a matter of physical recognition.

How, then, do we distill and recognize a person's identity from that person's many and varied actions, none of which may be exactly like any other? We do so by observing those actions, comparing them, and marking certain patterns of action. Over time, we correct or modify or enlarge our understanding on the basis of new observations and comparisons. Our conception of a person's identity is never final since the person is constantly performing new actions; yet, our conception is reliable because certain patterns of action become familiar.

In addition to this, we grasp a person's identity because we recognize every individual as like or unlike other persons. Jane is Jane because she is different from Jill or because she is like Joan. Without our complex sense of other persons we could not grasp the identity of a particular person. Not only this. We also imagine hypothetical situations to enrich our understanding of a person's identity. We imagine what a certain person would do in a certain situation, what it would be like to be another person or act as another person. We fantasize about other persons, real and imaginary, as a means for understanding others and ourselves. We are constantly creating models of persons and modifying and enriching our models in an effort to gain ever more confident understanding.

This account of the process of understanding will help us grasp what is involved in the understanding of texts. All actions are historical, occurring in time and having a temporal structure; understanding occurs when we see the relation of prior acts and prior moments to subsequent acts and subsequent moments. Such is the case even for our understanding of mathematical and logical propositions, for such propositions cannot be understood discretely but only in relation to our prior understanding of related propositions. The relations themselves among logical propositions are atemporal and exist apart from human acts of understanding, but our understanding of them can only be grasped as a process of discovering, proposing, testing, accepting, or rejecting. Understanding, in short, occurs as a temporal process wherein new propositions are proposed and tested in relation to propositions which are already familiar. New theories, as Thomas Kuhn and others point out, can be proposed and evaluated only in the context of theories already held: such is the condition which history places on understanding.

If the historicity of action implies that all understanding is based on a relation of resemblance between the new and the familiar, then all understanding is also dynamic or progressive. Every moment introduces new perceptions and contexts in which the new and the familiar are continuously interacting. Usually these interactions are so pervasively regulated by conventions and habits that we hardly notice the constantly changing patterns of our experiences and thoughts; nevertheless, we are constantly absorbing, evaluating, and using new experiences. And we do so by relating them, consciously or not, to the patterns of experience which we have previously developed.

We may describe this as a process of *modeling*. Most of our models for action are conventional; we simply do things as we have become accustomed to do them. But if we modify the typical patterns of our actions, we do so by imagining and choosing among alternative possibilities for action. Our choices may range from the automatic to the deliberately self-conscious, but in every case a pattern of relationships or a *model* for action is operative. Without such models our actions would be random and purposeless.

The process of understanding we have described also operates in our understanding of fictional texts. We imagine fictional worlds in order to gain a richer understanding of our actual world. Fictional worlds function as models whereby we explore the possibilities of understanding and living in the world. Without a familiar or given sense of what the world is like, we could not imagine new possibilities, but without the ability to imagine new possibilities we could not expand our understanding or use it creatively.

If fictional worlds have a mimetic relationship to the actual world and function as models do, then fictional works serve us as interpretations of the actual world. Fiction is itself hermeneutical; it offers new ways of "seeing" or interpreting the world. And if this is so, fictional works also serve a heuristic purpose; they open up for us new ways of reflecting on the world. To interpret fiction hermeneutically is also to use fiction heuristically as a means for helping us to understand the world in which we are always living and acting. Every fictional text implies the question "What if the world were like this?" We reflect upon fictional worlds as alternatives to the actual world, and our interpretation of their significance helps us to reflect on the significance of the actual world. In this way works of fiction present us with new models for our thinking about the actual world. They become meaningful to us because we are able to compare their fictional worlds with the world that is already familiar to us.

Our understanding of texts and our comparing of worlds are often intuitive and not self-conscious activities. Much of our understanding of texts, in fact, is pretheoretical in the sense that it does not involve problems which need to be mediated by self-conscious hermeneutical methods. A large body of traditional and shared experience shapes our intuitional or pretheoretical understanding of texts, and this body of understanding provides the context for our more self-conscious efforts to understand when we encounter or raise interpretive problems. Often, then, we may understand a work of fiction and its significance, to a degree at least, without having to engage in self-conscious hermeneutical analysis. But because fictional worlds are mimetically related to the actual world, we are always *able* to use fictional texts as a means for self-consciously reflecting on the fictional world and its relationship to the actual world. Fiction is interesting and valuable for us not only because we enjoy imaginative activities and aesthetic experiences but also because a fictional text presents us with an alternative way of "seeing" the world.[52]

We are able to understand the events of a fictional story because we have encountered and witnessed numerous events, fictional or actual, in our previous experience. But whether the persons and events are fictional or actual makes no difference as far as the *processes* of understanding are concerned. The comparisons we make among objects and actions are not "world bound" but cut across the boundaries of worlds. We compare Huck Finn and Tom Sawyer to boys that we have known in actual life even though we have no doubts whatsoever which of the boys are fictional and which are actual. In this way fiction illuminates life and life illuminates fiction. Without the mimetic relationship, fiction could neither exist nor be of interest to us. Far from being autonomous worlds grounded in the autonomy of literary language, the worlds of fictional works derive their meaning and value from their anchorage in the actual world. We encounter fictional persons who live in fictional "worlds," and we discover that they are like (or unlike) us and that their worlds are like (or unlike) our world. And through the resemblance—through the mimesis—we discover the value of the encounter.[53]

Two further implications of this view help to clarify some issues pertaining to the creation of texts and the reading of texts. First, if we can imagine new possibilities only on the basis of what we already know, then new fictional "worlds" have a necessary relationship to the worlds already familiar to us. These familiar worlds may include some or all of the fictional worlds already projected by previous works of fiction, but they will certainly also include the actual world which every author inhabits. Only because authors have some knowledge of the actual world can they project a new fictional world. Although the fictional world is not a "copy" of the world familiar to the author (the case of fantasy would surely be enough to discredit a naive conception of mimesis), neither is it possible for the fictional world to exist apart from a mimetic relation to the familiar world.

This mimetic relationship is one of the reasons why historical considerations are part of hermeneutics. The way authors perceive the world and the way their perceptions are influenced by their historical situation shape the fictional worlds they are able to imagine and project. Historical matters will never absorb hermeneutics because we remain primarily interested in the fictional work and the world it projects. Nevertheless, our understanding of historical backgrounds—or the world behind the text—may often be illuminating and even necessary for an adequate understanding of the text.

A second implication concerns the reading of a text. If the new must be seen and understood in relation to the familiar, then for readers, too, the new world of a fictional text will inevitably be understood in relation to worlds already familiar, the fictional worlds they have previously encountered and the world they actually inhabit. Hermeneutics cannot escape the fact that texts are interpreted in the cultural contexts of readers. This does not make hermeneutics an entirely subjective or relativistic enterprise, but it does entail an important consequence for the reading and interpreting of texts: the task of hermeneutics can never be finished. The worlds of fiction cannot change (the world of Shakespeare's *Hamlet* is the same for all readers in all ages), but the way we interpret their relationship to the actual world is constantly changing because our interpretive contexts change. History makes hermeneutical tasks very complex, but if hermeneutics frustrates us by offering no end to the interpretive process, it also blesses us with the possibility of growth.

Some Consequences for Hermeneutical Practice

The first consequence is, of course, that texts are not to be approached as autonomous aesthetic objects. If they are objects and instruments of action, we must be alert to the many ways we use them. We use them to amuse us, to relax or stimulate us in various ways, to confirm or obstruct our beliefs, to force discipline on our children, to provide illustrations for our lectures, to reinforce our arguments in a debate, to give us source material for our scholarly work. But certainly one of the most common and important uses of texts is that of interpreting and understanding them. And this is the concern of hermeneutics. Hermeneutics is not, then, a general theory of all the uses of texts but of the understanding or interpretation of texts.

Since, as we have suggested, the fictional world stands in a mimetic relationship to the actual world, we examine the world of the text in ways that are similar to those we use in our examination of the actual world. If we adopt Marxist models in our analysis of actual societies, we tend to examine fictional societies also from a Marxist point of view. If we use Freudian models in our analysis of actual persons, we tend to use the Freudian models for our study of fictional persons. If we hold a Christian view of human actions, we will tend to view the actions of fictional characters in the light of Christian models. Because the mimetic value of literature lies precisely at the points at which fictional worlds resemble the actual world, we naturally adapt our models for understanding the actual world to our understanding of imagined worlds.

But is the "natural" tendency the proper one? If literature has a heuristic function, if it provides possibilities for imagining new models and alternative possibilities, is it not better to let the world of the work stand for what it is as a "new" model rather than to assimilate it into the models which we have already formulated? Should we not allow fictional worlds to challenge us and open us to new possibilities of thought rather than to fit them into preestablished categories?

It is possible, of course, to read *Moby Dick* as an existentialist novel or to find Freudian or Marxist or Christian patterns in it, but doesn't a responsible reading demand that we first attempt to understand the world of the novel as Melville presents it? Since the new is always understood by the already familiar, we cannot escape our tendency and our need to use familiar models in the hermeneutical process, but what is necessary is to remain as open as possible to the newness that confronts the familiar. Otherwise the value of literature for hermeneutics can be minimized or lost.

We can maintain an attitude of openness if we remain aware of the various levels of analysis which our approach to hermeneutics uncovers. At the first level we recognize that the author uses language in forming a text. Our understanding of the text, therefore, depends on our ability to understand the language and various linguistic devices. At this level we use some of the components of what W. K. Wimsatt has called "our inherited grammar of criticism":[54] we identify and describe the diction, imagery, metaphor, figures of speech and other rhetorical devices of prose or the meter, rhyme, alliteration, and other characteristic uses of language in poetry. Since the author patterns the language in a text, we also include at this level the formal designs in the work: plot, devices of characterization and description, stanzaic forms, style, and the like. When we analyze a text at this level, we are focusing on the formal elements of the text, not on the world that is projected by means of the text or on how the author is using these elements to give significance to the work. By itself this level of analysis is incomplete and must lead to other levels, but we note before going on that much of our pleasure in reading comes from the delight we take in experiencing the formal elements of a text. Indeed, the pleasure of reading is often simply the aesthetic delight we take in the formal artistry of the text.

At a second level of understanding we examine the imagined

world that the author projects in the language of the text. Our interest at this level is not so much the author's deployment of the language as it is the descriptive references of the language, the states of affairs it presents. Before we can go on to answer further questions about the meaning of the text, we must know what the text says, which in the case of narrative fiction is the story that is told. At this level we attempt to give an accurate accounting of the characters, events, and situations in a narrative text. Sometimes we think of this as the text's literal meaning—what it literally says. Because of the ambivalence of the term *literal,* however, it is better to speak of the states of affairs (the objects, events, actions, or situations) that are designated by the language. This analysis is sometimes controversial, as, for example, when we ask whether Jay Gatsby really loved Daisy Buchanan in Fitzgerald's *The Great Gatsby* or whether Ligeia came back to life in the body of Rowena in Poe's story "Ligeia." In such cases our interpretation of the evidence at this level will influence our interpretation at the other levels. With respect to most of the occurrences in a novel, however, most readers are in agreement.

When we move to a third level, we ask how an author gives significance to the world that the text projects. We ask, for example, questions about a character's motivation: why did Jay Gatsby pursue Daisy Buchanan, or why did Ligeia struggle against death? Such questions ask not just *what* happened but *why* it happened. At this level we must interpret the significance of what takes place in a narrative. *Significance* is another elusive term because it often suggests relativism in interpretation: significance for whom? We should distinguish clearly, therefore, between significance for the author and significance for the reader. Although we cannot totally separate these, many controversies occur because critics are too willing to conflate them.

A helpful discussion of how authors give significance to the worlds they project is found in Nicholas Wolterstorff's *Art in Action:*

> But what must now be noticed is that there is more to the workings and significance of his [the author's] use of those words than just that thereby he projects the world of the work. A simple way of putting the point is this: fictional discourse has significance beyond *story,* where "story" is understood as designating the world of the work. For one thing, not only does the discourse give us the story; it gives us the story *in a certain way.* But secondly, fictional discourse often bears a significance beyond even that of giving us the story in a certain way.[55]

By the phrase "gives us a story in a certain way" Wolterstorff means simply that the events which constitute the story may be told in different ways by different narrators without the story itself becoming a different story. Three eyewitness reports of a traffic accident, for example, will not be identical word-for-word, even if they are in essential agreement about what happened. Sophocles's *Antigone* and Anouilh's *Antigone* tell the same story, but each text tells the story "in a certain way." In any particular telling of a story, however, an author uses certain narrative strategies which indicate how he sees the significance of the story. These strategies constitute, in Wolterstorff's terminology, the text's point of view. By analyzing how these strategies function in a text, we move toward an understanding of the significance of the story from one author's point of view.

In formalist practice, the term *point of view* is typically used to designate only the "narrative voice" in a story; it identifies the "teller of the tale." Formalist critics often go on to assume that we need not inquire further into an authorial point of view, because the "narrative voice" belongs either to a character within the story or to an anonymous *persona* who is to be distinguished from the author of the text. But if the author of a text stands behind the work establishing *all* of its narrative strategies, then limiting the term *point of view* to the "narrative voice" of a character or *persona* can lead us to ignore or minimize the importance of the author's actions in forming a text. The issue here is partly one of preferred usage, but the formalist usage often hides the crucial issue of the author's presence in the text. To highlight this presence we might better use the term to include *all* the strategies an author uses to give significance to the story.

In addition to "narrative voice," or point of view in the narrow sense, the authorial point of view in the broader sense includes, as Wolterstorff observes, the following narrative strategies: the reliability or unreliability of the narrator; pacing, or the manipulation of the temporal order of the story; the knowledge/ignorance contour, or the giving and withholding of information; focus, or the highlighting or minimizing of details; evaluation, or the exhibition of authorial attitudes toward characters and events in the story; the use of symbols and of allusions to things and events which occur outside the projected world; and the expression of beliefs concerning the actual world.[56] Much of our understanding of a text depends on our alertness to these narrative strategies.

A fourth level in the analysis of fictional texts involves their mimetic function. In part our interpretation of the fictional world of a text rests on how we construe its mimetic relationship to the actual world. Since the fictional world is anchored in and bears a resemblance to the actual world, our methods of analyzing the fictional world are usually and understandably analogous to those we use for analyzing the actual world. But consequently our choice of methods and our theories or biases concerning methodologies are also reflected in the ways we analyze the mimetic function of texts.

The methods of analysis we use to understand the world around us are indicated by the familiar disciplines which appear in our universities. We examine the world as physicists, sociologists, psychologists, philosophers, or linguists, for example. Analogously we inquire into the psychological, social, political, ethical, or religious dimensions or implications of the world that is projected in a novel. To some extent various types of criticism can be understood as giving priority to one or more of these categories: Freudian criticism stresses the psychological level, Marxist the political-economic levels, Christian criticism the religious-ethical. Literature is amenable to these types of criticism because in literary works we are confronted with worlds which manifest the various dimensions of experience and reality.

One of the general concerns of hermeneutics, therefore, is uncovering the relationships among the many dimensions of our experience. One interesting view of how this concern can operate can be found in the Dutch philosopher Herman Dooyeweerd. Dooyeweerd suggests that we may discover in our experience of the world at least fourteen modalities or dimensions. Among them are, for example, the ethical, jural, aesthetic, economic, social, and historical. In his view our analysis of the world can be pursued at any of these levels, but a *full* analysis would have to consider all of them in their varied relationships.[57] Dooyeweerd also posits the need for a unifying or organizing principle in any systematizing theory of knowledge, the kind of unifying principle that Frederic Jameson is seeking in *The Political Unconscious.* For Dooyeweerd this organizing principle is religious; he identifies it as the relationship of people in their innermost being to God. Human actions at the various levels of experience are, in his view, manifestations of the ways in which people live out, ariculate, explore, affirm, or deny their identity as creatures who in a fundamental sense are religious beings.

Aside from Dooyeweerd's own philosophy, however, his schematic paradigm of levels, structured in relation to some unifying conception of experience, points up issues that confront a theory of how we analyze the dimensions of the worlds presented to us in fictional works. For us to interpret a fictional world at the mimetic level, we need some kind of systematizing theory of the nature and kinds of human actions. Such a comprehensive theory—whether Marxist, Freudian, Christian, or other—is necessary as we strive for a full understanding of what it is to interpret a world. Our own view of the structure and unity of life will shape the way we interpret the worlds of fictional texts.

Complications appear at this level of analysis, however, even aside from the problem of our own methodological biases and theories. One of these is that fictional worlds are never given in their full extension but are what Wolterstorff calls "world segments." This means that an author may, by a selection of material, choose to highlight one aspect or dimension of experience and ignore others. When an author highlights certain aspects of experience, as Poe, for example, highlights psychological terror, we may not conclude from that fact that he fails to recognize or acknowledge other dimensions of experience. We may not, for example, conclude that Poe highlights psychological terror because he is insufficiently aware of the religious dimensions of life. A conclusion such as that would depend on our assessment of the scope of Poe's work, of his principles of selection, of his authorial point of view, and of all the other levels of analysis. Because our analysis of texts at the level of their mimetic function depends on our own conception of the dimensions of experience and the appropriate methods of analysis, we are highly susceptible to hasty interpretive generalizations. Determining the scope of the text's world segment is one check on our tendency to generalize too broadly.

But in spite of the difficulties at this level, the mimetic function of texts also opens up and enables us to understand a fifth level of interpretation, that of evaluation. We do not mean only aesthetic evaluation, which is our judgment about the author's artistry in forming the text, but also evaluation of the world the work projects and the significance it derives from the authorial point of view. Our evaluation emerges in a natural way from the mimetic relationship of fictional world to actual world: we naturally and perhaps inevitably draw comparisons between the world of the text and the world we inhabit. We encounter the new perspectives and paradigms presented in the text and grasp them in the light of those already familiar to us.

Because the narrative text has a point of view as well as a world, the author interprets as well as projects the world or world segment. Thereby the author develops his or her themes and, if the scope of the world is large, forms an entire worldview, that is to say, a view of the fictional world. Because the mimetic function of the text brings the author's views into relation with our own as readers, the understanding of a text is not complete until this relationship of meaning is explored. The fact that different readers will hold different worldviews means, of course, that evaluations will differ. But that is no reason to eliminate evaluation from the task of hermeneutics. Our aim is not only to understand Hemingway's themes and worldview but also to evaluate them. Literature confronts us with new ways of seeing the world, and only when we take the step of evaluating the world of the work and the way the author presents it to us do we claim the full value of literature for our lives as human beings. In this way the interpretation of literature helps us to interpret the world in which we live from day to day.

None of the levels of analysis we have distinguished can be isolated from the others, and therefore the term *levels* is misleading as well as useful. One reason why the goal of hermeneutics cannot be the identification of a single valid and verifiable textual meaning is that some of these levels involve our personal philosophies, and these levels cannot be detached from the others. The distinguishing of levels, however, can encourage an attitude of openness toward the possibilities of interpretation and show us how our personal philosophies enter the process of understanding.

At this point it may be useful to summarize the levels we have discussed before we go on to two related topics:

1. Through the deployment of language, the author forms a text. At this level we analyze the formal features of a text.

2. Through the descriptive references of the language, the author projects an imagined world. At this level we aim accurately to survey the details, structure, and scope of the fictional world.

3. Through the use of narrative strategies, the author establishes a point of view. At this level we try to understand how the author gives significance to the imagined world, how he or she interprets it.

4. Through its anchorage in the actual world, the fictional world acquires a mimetic function. At this level we compare the fictional world to the actual world, inescapably employing the models we use in our understanding of the actual world.

5. Through its linguistic form, its projected world, its point of view, and its mimetic function, the text presents us with a model or paradigmatic way of viewing the world or some aspect of it. At this level we evaluate the text and what it has to say.[58]

The actual process of interpretation, of course, is not as simple or schematic as this summary makes it appear.

So far the levels we have distinguished involve the author's actions in projecting an imagined world by way of inscribing a text and the reader's actions in interpreting the world that is projected. They have been concerned with the text as an *object* produced by the author's actions. But two additional levels of meaning have a bearing on this hermeneutical process. These concern the possible uses of the text as an *instrument* or means for performing additional actions. Some of these instrumental uses may be pertinent to our understanding of the text as an object.

A sixth level, therefore, is indicated by the fact that authors may use the text to earn an income, to influence or compete with their peers, or to secure the favor of a benefactor. Or, less crassly, they may do so to entertain their readers, to counsel their followers, to express their creative visions. Here we are speaking not just of the significance authors give to the world projected by the text, but the significance for authors of the text as an object that they produce.

Of these innumerable ends for which authors can use a text, few, if any, are evident from the text alone; they will usually be discovered as the result of historical research or historical reconstruction. Often, though, knowledge of such ends will be helpful and sometimes even crucial for our understanding. It is crucial, for example, as the next chapter shows, to use historical reconstruction to help us understand the social or teaching function of the parables of Jesus and to use that knowledge to help us interpret their meaning at other levels of significance. But although many of these uses of texts will be important for interpretation, many will also be irrelevant or insignificant. How significant, for example, for our understanding of James Fennimore Cooper's first novel is our knowledge that he wrote it to show he could write a better novel than the ones he had been reading? At this level of interpretation much depends on the critic's judgments about the historical circumstances surrounding the author's forming of the text.

Similarly a seventh level becomes evident when we observe the ways in which readers use texts. We may use them to impress others with our erudition, to while away our spare hours, or to promote our professional goals. Or we may use them to vindicate our own philosophies, to assist our acts of worship, or to console us in stressful times. These uses may be irrelevant for our understanding of a text or may at times be significant. For example, the use of the Bible to focus and confirm the religious practices of the church is highly relevant to the ways we interpret the biblical text. Indeed, whenever we use a text to confirm or modify social practices, our uses will play an important role in the way we interpret the text's world and its point of view. Often this level of interpretation is a decisive one for hermeneutics.

Historical Texts

Although our discussion has focused on problems of fictional texts, our theory, if it is a useful one, should also be applicable to nonliterary or nonfictional texts. We turn, therefore, to a brief look at how we might deal with three questions raised by historical texts. Historical texts are like fictional texts in that they are basically narrative in structure and thus project worlds, but they differ in that they are not used to project fictional or imagined worlds. Historical texts are used to make claims about the actual world. In distinguishing historical from fictional texts, therefore, we need an additional concept—that of authorial stance—to specify the kinds of claims that are being made by different types of texts. Let us call the stance of the historian the *assertive* stance and contrast it to the *fictional* stance of a novelist. The assertive stance of the historian embraces an interpretation and evaluation of certain data as well as a narrative or descriptive account of the data. What interests us in a historical text is that the historian claims—asserts—that the projected world (the story) of the text together with the authorial point of view counts as a story and an interpretation of events as they actually occurred. Such is obviously not the claim of the writer of fiction. We are, of course, interested in the projected world of the historical text, but our primary interest focuses ordinarily on whether the projected world of the text in fact coincides with the actual world.[59]

The first question we raise is this: how do we account for historical errors in works which claim to describe the actual world? In the case of fictional works there can be no errors since the imagined world is just exactly that world which the author projects by means of the text. But if we have varying accounts of actual historical events, some of which are shown to include errors of fact, can those accounts which contain errors be accurately classified as historical works? Or must historical works which include errors be considered partly historical and partly fictional?

This question may seem trivial, a matter of personal choice in classification or definition. But it is related to other, more fundamental questions about factuality and truth to be raised later. The question whether erroneous statements in a historical text are to be considered fictional statements rather than historical statements is a question concerning the kind of text we have in hand,[60] and in ordinary contexts such questions are determined on the basis of authorial stance rather than on the basis of the truth or factuality of references. When we read a historical text, such as Gibbon's *The Decline and Fall of the Roman Empire,* we do not in practice make our judgment about the kind of text it is (history or fiction) depend on the accuracy or truth of every detail. We classify Gibbon's work as a historical work even if we happen to find in it some factual errors.

The same holds true for the individual statements in a text. If a work clearly identifiable as a historical text contains an erroneous statement, even that statement is taken to be a historical statement, or a historical-type-of-statement. If, for example, a historian writes "General X led his troops to victory at Three-Surfers Peak," and it turns out that Colonel X was later promoted to General only after this victory, we would not be compelled to regard the erroneous statement as a kind of fictional statement. The author was claiming (asserting) that this statement, along with all the other statements in the text, was to count as historical description. The fact that the author was subsequently shown to be in error does not in practice induce us to change our judgment about the kind of text or the kind of statement. We continue to regard a text as historical even though it may contain errors of fact, just as we continue to regard a novel as fiction even though it may include factual references to actual events or personages.

This does not mean that a writer can deliberately "invent" a story and pass it off as history, for in so doing the author assumes the stance of a counterfeiter rather than a historian. The case of Clifford Irving's biography of Howard Hughes is a good example. Before Irving's book was exposed as a fabrication, we would have taken it as a historical text—but not afterward. On what criteria is this judgment based? Certainly it is not based on our scrutiny of every detail of the biography and our judgment concerning how much is factual and how much in error. Rather, once Irving's "authorial stance" became clear, the text could not be taken as a historical work even if it did include some or many factual statements. The accuracy or erroneousness of statements is one of the clues we use to discover or recognize authorial stance, but our judgment about the kind of text is determined by our judgment about authorial stance.

Many of the fascinating marginal texts which make classification of kinds and genres difficult as well as interesting involve deliberate experiments with authorial stance. Irony, satire, parody, as well as deliberate ruse, depend on authorial stance. Often the stance can be detected only by the clues we have concerning the accuracy of the descriptive details which the author gives us, but the kind or genre of the text remains in doubt until we arrive at some judgment about the stance. Washington Irving's *Knickerbocker History of New York,* for example, achieves its satirical effect by Irving's pretended use of a historian's stance in narrating events which are clearly not actual events. Much science fiction, too, simulates a historian's stance with respect to imagined events at some future time. Similarly, satirical works such as Dryden's "MacFlecknoe" or Franklin's "The Sale of the Hessians" would never be classified as historical works even though the statements included in them refer to actual events, for the stance of Dryden and Franklin is not that of the historian but of the satirist. In all these marginal cases, as well as in other genres such as autobiography, journalistic reporting, historical fiction, and the like, our classifications are related to questions of authorial stance.

With respect to ordinary (nonmarginal) historical texts the historian's stance is generally clear, and such texts are taken to be historical even when errors are discovered in them. To regard such texts as a mixture of history and fiction would be to confuse the way in which kinds of texts are identified and to overlook the crucial role played by the authorial stance in our classification of them. As we have observed, an author's stance is not always immediately clear, and it may be complicated; nevertheless, we take as historical works those which in good faith exhibit a historian's stance. Historical errors are simply incorrect statements about the actual world which do (occasionally) appear in historical texts.

A second question arises when we pursue our first one a little further. How do we determine the kind or class of a particular text when the authorial stance is not immediately clear? Here we focus more fully on the ways we identify the class of a particular text rather than on the definition of the kinds of texts or on the kinds of statements that can be included in various texts. We have just suggested how it is in general that historical works can include statements which are in error and that fictional works can include statements which are accurate with respect to actual events; in both cases this is possible because our *definition* of various kinds of texts is based on the authorial stance adopted by the author, not on the states of affairs *per se*. But we have not yet clarified how we go about discovering what the authorial stance is in a particular text.

Let us examine this question by considering the relationship of history to legends and historical fiction. Legends are generally thought to be fictional elaborations on historical events, and historical fictions are generally considered to have a historical factuality which is filled out by the addition of fictional events compatible in spirit with actual events. This confirms our earlier point that kinds of texts are not rigidly defined in terms of the factual accuracy of the worlds they present. Factually accurate references may be included in fictional works, and fictional elements are included in legends and historical novels.

In cases where the authorial stance is not immediately obvious, how do we recognize and identify the class of a text? The answer appears to be threefold. First, we do consider whether the world that is given by the text is factually accurate. Our analysis in this regard depends in part on our criteria for judging whether the objects and events that constitute the world of the text actually occurred. Second, every text exhibits a point of view as well as a description of certain states of affairs. The author's techniques of presentation often serve as indications of the kind of text that we are dealing with. Third, texts are used for certain purposes, and the purpose of a text is determined not just by the authorial point of view but also by the ways texts are used by authors and readers. In most cases we recognize the class of a text simply by knowing something about the author and the circumstances surrounding the writing and publishing of it, but in some cases, particularly in the case of anonymous texts, we may have to examine one or all of the criteria mentioned.

Examining these criteria we observe, first, that with respect to its factual accuracy the identification of a text as historical or fictional is usually clear. *Huckleberry Finn* is clearly fictional even though the fictional world of the novel exhibits certain resemblances to the actual world, whereas Allan Nevin's *The War for the Union* is clearly a historical account of the American Civil War. A work like Crane's The *Red Badge of Courage* is clearly fictional even though its plot bears a close resemblance to the events of the battle of Chancellorsville, whereas William Gilmore Simms's *The Forayers* is recognized as historical fiction since it includes recognizable historical figures and actions in the context of a fictionalized story of the Revolutionary War. In certain cases, however, the factuality of texts is harder to determine. Many of the stories about Davy

Crockett, for example, are not wholly factual even though they are based on the historical figure of David Crockett, the American pioneer and politician. Some of these stories that may once have been told as factual and taken as historical are now judged to be legendary rather than historical. Thus, when we ask "What is the authorial stance in this text?" we may in the first instance seek to determine whether the objects and events in the text are actual historical events. At this level, the task of classification raises questions concerning historical methodology and historical reconstruction. We take as factual those events which our operative criteria establish as factual or as probably factual.

The second set of criteria involves authorial point of view, that is, the ways in which narrative techniques give significance to the worlds projected by texts. These techniques, which are many and varied, continue to be among the central concerns of "genre" and "structuralist" criticism. They involve not only such techniques as conventional or formulaic phrasing, genealogical catalogs, and the use of hyperbole and careful documentation but also less obvious structural patterns involving beginnings and endings, uses of metaphor, symbol, and allusion, sequences of events, and chronological ordering. Northrop Frye's work demonstrates how the investigation of formal techniques reveals a work's point of view and establishes its genre classification.

The third set of criteria concerns the uses that are made of these types of texts. At this level we inquire whether given texts are used for acquiring knowledge of past events, providing patriotic celebration of national heroes, interpreting social experience, and the like, and we tend to associate certain of these functions with certain kinds of texts.

Since we are not in this discussion attempting to specify the difference among kinds of texts but only to suggest what hermeneutical factors are involved in their identification, we may summarize our suggestions so far as follows: the types of texts which we identify, and which in turn help shape the hermeneutical issues and approaches which are pertinent to each, are defined in relation to the stances which authors adopt in their presentations. In most cases an author's stance will be known or easily recognized, but in many cases the stance will be either deliberately complicated or, for historical or sociological reasons, difficult to determine. The determination of the authorial stance and the kind of the work will then depend on our judgments about three textual concerns: the accuracy of descriptive references, the authorial point of view, and the function or use of the text by its audience.

A third question often confuses attempts to formulate a general theory of texts and textual interpretation: How is the distinction between truth and falsity related to the distinction between history and fiction? One of the persistent misconceptions of textual hermeneutics is the correlation of the truth-falsity distinction with the history-fiction distinction. What is historical and actual is taken to be truthful, and therefore what is fictional and imagined is thought to be false. When and why this popular disjunction made its appearance in the history of hermeneutical thinking would be an interesting and illuminating study; that it did so is one of the unfortunate developments in the intellectual history of the West.

The nature of the problem can be assessed as follows. It stems from the isolation of the states of affairs that are being described or presented by a text from the authorial point of view and from the uses of the text. The common view assumes that historical texts are true since the events being described actually took place. On the other hand, since the states of affairs in a work of fiction do not occur in the actual world, the same common view assumes that fictional texts must be false. In both cases the question of truth or falsity is focused exclusively on the states of affairs that the text presents.

In raising this question we do not want to address general epistemological questions concerning the nature of truth and of truth-claims, though they lie in the background of our discussion. We want only to try to clarify certain hermeneutical problems relating to truth in historical and fictional texts. We may begin, therefore, with the observation that our judgments about the truth or falsity of a text must take into account the complex interrelation of the world of the text (the states of affairs being presented), the authorial point of view, the authorial stance, and the purposes for which the author may be using the text.

First, for a historian to adopt a historical stance is to claim that the states of affairs presented in the text coincide with actual states of affairs. Here we encounter several problems. The truth of the historian's claims depends on whether the states of affairs the text presents coincide with the way the world actually is or was. But since the actual states of affairs the historian claims to describe have slipped away into the past (except for surviving artifacts), he or she cannot observe them directly. At best, therefore, the historian can have only *beliefs* about past states of affairs, if belief is contrasted here to direct observation. With respect to historical claims, the question of truth and falsity becomes the question of justified beliefs. We need, consequently, to raise the problem of what criteria we use to test the truth of a historical claim. These criteria pertain to the proper use of evidence, and this, in turn, involves our conception of the nature of evidence and the means for discovering it. Hence, the criteria we use to judge the truth of historical claims about the occurrence of events and situations are, in the final analysis, established by the cultural practices and methodologies we use in carrying on historical research. We accept as historically true those statements which our historiographical skills justify us in believing true.

The world projected by the fictional text, however, does not (by and large) coincide with actual events, and the fiction writer does not claim that they do. If therefore we define as true those states of affairs that actually occur and as false those that do not, then we must say that the fiction writer projects for us false or nonoccurring states of affairs as opposed to the true or occurring affairs proffered by an accurate historian.

But in practice we do not restrict the terms *true* and *false* just to the states of affairs presented in a text. We use them also to characterize the assertions that are made by the statements in a text. In fact, we speak of *true* or *false* assertions even more commonly than we do of true or false states of affairs. This is what lies behind Sir Philip Sidney's well-known remark that poets never tell lies. Sidney was observing that (using our terminology) poets in their fictions never make truth-claims about the occurrence of actual states of affairs; that is, since poets make no *assertions* about the actual world, they speak no falsehoods. He did not think of truth or falsehood as a measure of whether the states of affairs in fiction actually occur or not—in which case he would have to say the poet's fictions are false.

When we examine questions of truth and falsity in relation to assertions, we must consider the role of authorial point of view, that is, the narrative strategies whereby the author gives significance to the world of the text. In the case of historical texts, the point of view establishes the historian's interpretation of the events and situations projected in the text, but it also functions in tandem with the authorial stance to establish the claim that the interpretation is an interpretation of events which have actually occurred. In a historical text, therefore, we encounter not only the author's interpretation of the events but also the claim that the events being interpreted were actual events. The author's statements count as interpretive assertions about actual events.

In contrast, the fiction writer's point of view establishes the author's interpretation of the events and situations that occur in the imagined world of the text, but since the author's stance makes or implies no claims about *actual* events and situations, point of view in fiction does not raise questions of truth or falsity. The fiction writer, by establishing an author's point of view, interprets or gives significance to the world projected in the text, but that interpretation pertains only to the fictional world and makes no assertions about the actual world. Historians make truth-claims both about the events they describe and the interpretation they place on those events. Fiction writers, however, make no truth-claims about the events in their text, and therefore their authorial point of view, their way of shaping and interpreting imagined events, does not carry with it any assertions about the actual world. Neither on the grounds of the states of affairs they present nor on the grounds of their authorial point of view do fiction writers say or imply anything true about the actual world.

But at this point we see the significance of the fourth of our key factors, the uses that authors can make of the texts they produce. In the case of the historian the primary use is implicit in the authorial stance: the writer is using the text in order to make claims about the actual world. In the case of the fiction writer the authorial stance implies that the primary use of the text is to project an imagined world. But texts can be used for other purposes, too, and in most cases writers of fiction do have additional uses for their texts. They may use their fictions as a means for making assertions or claims about the actual world even though the individual sentences of their fictions do not, generally speaking, make truth-claims about the occurrence of actual states of affairs.

For example, it is generally agreed that in his novels Faulkner is saying (or implying) that a burden of guilt hangs over his native South because of the the history of slavery and segregation in the southern states. Nothing in his novels, however, says this directly. Rather, the sentences of the novels pertain to characters and events which are by and large purely imaginary and do not make claims about the occurrence of actual states of affairs. Yet Faulkner can (and probably does) use these novels as a means for making assertions about the actual world; the novels may *count as* assertions about the actual world. These implied assertions or claims, when they are identified or determined, become subject to the criteria we have for truth and falsity, for they are interpretive claims about actual states of affairs. In fiction, then, authors use their texts to project an imagined world, but they can also use their texts to assert something about the actual world. They may do so explicitly in the text, but ordinarily they will do so by implying or suggesting by their choice of narrative strategies certain relationships which they see between the imagined world and the actual world. Of course, fiction writers need not be interested in such uses at all; some may write just to entertain.

These observations explain why the truth-falsity distinction is not parallel to the history-fiction distinction. Legends and novels, as well as historical texts, can be used to assert something about the actual world, and what they assert may be true or false. Sometimes we say that a legend is true, meaning that it is based on or includes historical fact. In this case we are asking whether the events of the story coincide with actual events—whether the world of the text counts as an accurate description of the actual world. At other times we say that a legend is true, meaning that what a legend says thematically about the world is true. In this case we are asking whether the legend is being used to assert something that is true. A fictional work can assert a truth by the telling of a story even though it does not give us factual references.

A hermeneutical theory which distinguishes between the world of the text and the actual world, between inscribing a text and taking an authorial stance, between projecting and asserting, between reference and mimesis will help to cut through those Gordian knots which have tied together history, referentiality, reality, and truth on the one hand and opposed them to fiction, nonreferentiality, imagination, and falsity on the other. Instead of separating history from fiction, reality from imagination, truth from fantasy, it is more accurate to conceive of history and fiction as related kinds of texts which can be both true and false in some respect or in some degree.

In both historical and fictional texts authors use language and narrative strategies to project worlds and to give significance to those worlds. The difference between them lies in their differing authorial stances and their differing functions or uses. In our account of these uses and of the other actions authors perform in inscribing texts, we have elaborated a hermeneutical model which shows the common structure of fictional and historical texts and provides principles for distinguishing between them.

III

READER-RESPONSE
HERMENEUTICS,
ACTION MODELS, AND
THE PARABLES OF JESUS

Anthony C. Thiselton

Literary Theory and Biblical Hermeneutics

What has biblical hermeneutics to do with literary theory? The two disciplines are not coextensive. Nor is biblical interpretation solely and without remainder a subcategory within literary theory, as if the Bible were no more than a particular example of literature which raised no distinctive theological questions. But at the very least, the theories of biblical and literary interpretation share much in common. Indeed we might even claim more. Most, if not all, of the broader questions raised in literary theory have some bearing on issues in biblical interpretation, even though, because the Christian community regards the Bible as its rule of faith, biblical hermeneutics also raises additional theological questions of its own.

The once popular notion that the chief hermeneutical difference between the Bible and literature depended on questions about facts, reference, and extralinguistic reality rests on simplistic assumptions both about literature and about the Bible.[1] For example many of the parables of Jesus, and perhaps the stories of Jonah or Job, function as fictional narratives. It does not matter to the interpretation of the parable of the good Samaritan whether a particular Samaritan once did the actions portrayed in the parable, though it does matter that the story points beyond itself to truth about God's grace, or to a certain understanding about the status of Israel or what it means to be a "neighbor." As for literature, important questions about how the fictional worlds of narrative refer beyond language itself remain central issues for literary theory. Literature, as Clarence Walhout has already pointed out, does more than present a self-contained or self-referring linguistic world. Nor, as Roger Lundin has urged, can we merely assert that literature provides primarily aesthetic pleasure while the Bible instructs us in matters of righteousness or truth. Neither in terms of their functions nor in terms of their relation to extralinguistic states of affairs can we posit a relation of mutual exclusion between the areas of literary and biblical hermeneutics. On the practical level moreover, quite apart from theological or literary theory, questions about the function of narrative, the temporal dimension of texts and their actions, and the role and status of the reader are all equally relevant to biblical and literary hermeneutics.

On the other hand, the special status accorded to the biblical text by the Christian community poses additional questions for the biblical interpreter and heightens the importance of certain shared concerns. In the Protestant tradition since the Reformation, a central concern of biblical hermeneutics has been that the interpreter allows the text of Scripture to control and mold his or her own judgments and does not subordinate the text to the interpretive tradition to which the interpreter belongs. The interpreter must somehow be prevented from finding in the text only what he or she is already expecting or hoping to find. A responsible hermeneutics will do something to prevent a shallow skimming from the text of the preformed viewpoints of the interpreter, now deceptively and dangerously clothed in the vestments of the authority of the text. Since in actual practice communities have sometimes shaped their lives and beliefs on the basis of what purport to be "biblical" truth but in fact have turned out to be bizarre distortions of it, biblical hermeneutics is of necessity a more anxious, more cautious, discipline than literary theory.

At either extreme of the spectrum between the cautious and the progressive, biblical hermeneutics can be negative and threatening. At the cautious end of the spectrum the discipline can become allied with a theological conservatism which reduces hermeneutics to a purely defensive device for maintaining the status quo of the interpretive procedures of a religious community. Under the guise of an objectivist view of this text, this approach simply assumes no difference between a "common sense" interpretive tradition and what the text itself says. In the interests of supposed safety, the interpretive tradition of the past is made into an inseparable part of the text itself, and openness to new truth and to correction *by* the text is suppressed.

At the same time, however, a supposedly progressive herme-neutics may be no less negative and threatening, if pressed to an equal extreme in the other direction. The demand for new tools, new perspectives, and new models may seem to suggest the gross inade-quacy of all the interpretive procedures of the past. In particular, valid insights about the role of the reader in literary and philosophical hermeneutics are sometimes pressed in such a way as to imply an infinite relativism on the part of the text or its author. Questions about meaning are reduced entirely to questions about language-effect in the modern world.

Neither of these extremes, however, is credible or acceptable. A hermeneutics which merely looks to past tradition, or defends the status quo, thereby shrugs off one of the most pertinent questions of our time. We no longer live in a situation (if we ever did) when only evangelical or orthodox Christians claim to be "biblical" in their thinking and practice. Recent debates in Christology have put orthodox Christians on the defensive, while so-called radical theologians claim to be more faithful to the Christology of Jesus, Paul, and even the whole New Testament than a Christendom which has been conditioned to read phrases like "Son of God" or "God sent . . ." within the framework of Western metaphysical categories. For the sake of both Christian witness and intellectual integrity we must ask how to determine whether that which molds the life of a given Christian community is actually the Bible or simply a particular interpretation of the Bible mediated through selective and privi-leged ways of understanding and using the text. Faithfulness to the Reformation entails the principle "ecclesia reformata semper refor-manda"; a reform which is never completed once-and-for-all, but which is renewed and reapplied from generation to generation in the light of Scripture. This calls for a hermeneutics which stands over against simply what is taken for granted in church tradition, and which, like the reformers and the prophets before them, asks ques-tions that are self-critical and uncomfortable.

At the same time, the exploration of new models and interpretive paradigms does not necessarily call in question the adequacy of past practices. Adequacy is always to be judged in relation to some goal. The concern to move forward does not cast doubt on the genuine sincerity of past faith or devotion, but it does entail a courageous grasp of every critical tool which may help the interpreter toward greater hermeneutical sensitivity, and therefore to greater faithfulness to the message of the text. Adequacy is always relative both to the resources available and to the goals to be achieved.

The interrelation of literary and biblical hermeneutics, however, also brings into focus a more positive and significant issue. The very contrast between hermeneutics and exegesis tempts the theorist to move beyond the level of exegetical particularity into more grandiose theorizing about generalities. In one sense it is inevitable that hermeneutics concerns generality. Walhout, for example, quite properly considers textuality as a general phenomenon in this volume. Lundin contrasts a horizon of expectation that is basically Cartesian with one that is more generally concerned with personal appropriation and ethical transformation. Nevertheless hermeneutics concerns the interpretation of texts produced during specific periods of time and how these are to be understood by readers who are also situated in time. Hermeneutical theories which reflect what Wittgenstein termed a craving for generality and a contemptuous attitude toward the particular case will founder on specific examples of particular texts.

Biblical studies as a discipline reflects a rigorous and meticulous concern for detailed questions about historical situations, types of texts, and the purpose and intended audience of given texts. In this respect it provides a salutary safeguard against more ambitious but less realistic conceptions of hermeneutics as somehow beyond questions about authors, situations, genre, readers, parallels, linguistic conventions, or temporal distance. Such an elevated regard for hermeneutics views such concepts as *general* categories, as if for example the author means *any* author of *any* text (not *this* author of *this* text). Questions about how important or unimportant the author of a text may be are treated to the same generalized answer regardless of whether we are talking about wisdom literature, the Pauline epistles, apocalyptic, or a piece of English literature.

Nothing could be more disastrous an assumption in practice. The present self-consciousness of our own academic generation about language and texts holds out great promise for our subject. But it also may seduce us into rushing prematurely into adopting monolithic and monochrome models of interpretation. We see the inadequacies of formalism in literary theory or of mere historical reconstruction in biblical studies and are tempted to embrace some alternative overarching model as the new key to the old problem. But François Bovon is correct: when we have rushed from reading "the text first in itself, understood for itself, apart from all reference to an author" and have moved toward a reflection on our status as readers, eventually we come to see that progress in hermeneutics comes along with the recognition that "diverse ways of access are possible, and that each one reveals an aspect of the landscape. A text does not have a single door nor a single key."[2] The adequacy or productiveness of each model or hermeneutical perspective proves itself not in generalizing debate, but in looking at the kind of text to which each interpretive model has special relevance. The confusions which bedevil many current hermeneutical discussions arise precisely because of the possibility of defending almost any model selected to study a paradigmatic case. Debate becomes mired when each side begins to view its own chosen paradigm as an overarching solution to *all* hermeneutical problems regardless of the kind of text in view or of the particular purpose for which the text is being read. Paradigms must be tested and if necessary modified in the actual process of interpreting particular texts, even if particular texts may also be served by the use of appropriate models and paradigms.

Surprisingly, the exponents of both literary and biblical hermeneutics seem slow to take to heart a lesson which has been thoroughly learned in several different philosophical traditions. At the most empirical and concrete level, J. L. Austin makes this point about the phrase "the meaning of a word."[3] It is one thing, he urges, to speak about the meaning of the word *X* (even the meaning of the word "word"), but it is quite another to speak about the meaning-of-a-word-in-general. This is simply to invite confusion. We might as well inquire what it would be to "attempt" something without asking concretely whether we are thinking of what it would be like to "attempt" to lift a heavy weight or to "attempt" to make a calculation or to "attempt" to go to sleep. Even if we can give some kind of general answer, such an answer will not necessarily succeed in calling attention to the major point at issue. It is (to use an example from Wittgenstein) as if we were to answer questions about the rise in butter prices by looking closely at the chemical constituency of butter rather than by asking questions about the economic situation. "The confusions which occupy us arise when language is like an engine idling, not when it is doing work."[4]

Heidegger's thought points in the same direction, even though he has come to the problem from quite a different angle. Interpretation, he urges, takes the form which it does only within a particular contextualized world and in the light of particular purposes. He brings this point to a focus in his category of "projection," or the dimension "for-the-sake-of-which."[5] This is why we propose to examine questions surrounding the interpretation of certain specific texts, namely the parables of Jesus, as a focus for our present hermeneutical inquiry.

The Parables of Jesus

The example of the parables of Jesus is instructive, in the first place, because Jesus himself underlines the need for some interpretive act or process on the part of the hearer if the parables are to achieve their effect. If the meaning of every parable were immediately apparent, why then did the disciples inquire about their interpretation (Mark 4:10-20; parallel Matthew 13:10-23, Luke 8:8-15)? Indeed Adolf Jülicher could insist on the obviousness of their meaning only by regarding all evidence in the Gospels to the contrary as inauthentic and misconceived constructions of the evangelists mistakenly or deliberately read back on to the lips of Jesus or into the original situation.[6]

Jülicher's fundamental mistake, however, was to presuppose that all parables performed the same hermeneutical function, namely that of illustrating certain broad and general truths which the Jesus of nineteenth-century theological liberalism was thought to teach. The lesson for biblical hermeneutics is that interpreters should not presuppose the so-called obviousness of any set of biblical texts in advance of actually considering their particular nature and function. It would be patently absurd, for example, to claim that Revelation or other instances of biblical apocalyptic held the same degree of supposed obviousness as, say, the book of Amos, although even this question cannot be answered apart from looking at the texts themselves. In the case of the parables, we may distinguish various subcategories within the form by examining degrees of open-endedness and levels of reader involvement.

At least three sets of variables determine the differences between these subcategories. They include differences of genre or hermeneutical function, differences of situation, and differences of audience—differences which naturally overlap. Jesus sometimes used example stories like that of the tower builder which do not entail the more complex transference of interpretive judgment to a second level characteristic of the parable form. Eta Linnemann comments, "In the parable the evaluation that the narrative compels one to make has to be carried over to another level (from 'picture' to 'reality'). In the illustration it refers directly to the reality and only needs to be generalized."[7] Bultmann makes the same kind of distinction: "Exemplary stories have a striking formal relationship to parables. . . . [They] offer examples, . . . models of right behavior."[8] In contrast to the subcategories of metaphor, similitude, and parable, Bultmann finds instances of such example stories in the good Samaritan, the rich fool, the rich man and Lazarus, and the Pharisee and the publican. But on closer inspection some of these, most notably the parable of the good Samaritan, reveal a more subtle and complex hermeneutical function. As J. D. Crossan rightly observes, if the purpose of this particular parable was to invite a Jewish audience to imitate the model of neighborly concern represented in the leading figure in the story, "for such a purpose it would have been far better to have made the wounded man Samaritan and the helper a Jewish man outside clerical circles."[9] To interpret this parable, we need a more adequate hermeneutical insight than that suggested by the subcategory of "example story."

One radical difference between example story and parable proper is in the sense of shock, disclosure, revelation, or reorientation which occurs in the case of the latter. Nathan's parable to David is a classic case. David becomes totally absorbed in Nathan's vivid portrayal of the rich man who took from the poor man the one thing that he had: "the poor man had . . . one little ewe lamb. . . . He brought it up, and it grew up with him and with his children; it used to eat of his morsel, and drink from his cup, and lie in his bosom, and it was like a daughter to him" (2 Samuel 12:3). As he sits on the edge of his chair, David feels righteous indignation when the rich man takes away the ewe lamb, and anger that the rich man "was unwilling to take one of his own flock or herd to prepare for the wayfarer who had come to him, but he took the poor man's lamb." The hermeneutical function of the parable is revealed in the close juxtaposition of two sentences. "David's anger was greatly kindled . . . and he said to Nathan, 'As the Lord lives, the man who has done this deserves to die . . . because he did this thing and because he had no pity.' Nathan said to David, 'You are the man' " (vv. 6, 7). Caught off guard by his involvement in the narrative world, David finds that the story is really about him before he has had the chance even to consider putting up moral defenses.

The difference between this kind of parable and the allegory is even more striking and fundamental. The reader can never be absorbed or "lost" in the world of the allegory in a way which conceals his or her own involvement in it. The parallels, applications, or relevance of the parts of an allegory are not experienced as a final, coherent surprise or revelation. Rather, they are a series of quasi-independent and repetitive or diffused correlations between the image and what the image represents that must be understood as the story proceeds. In Bunyan's *Pilgrim's Progress,* the reader knows that Christian's burden is really sin; that Mr. Worldly-Wiseman is a conceptual construct of worldly-wise people who impinge on Bunyan's and the reader's own lives; that the room in the house of the interpreter is really a human heart; that the oil poured on the fire is really the Holy Spirit; and so on. At each stage the reader is required to bring along an interpretive key. Interpretation of this sort is very different from what it is in the case of Nathan's parable.

We do not ask whether the ewe lamb is a good symbol for Uriah's wife; we discover that the relevance of any element in the narrative consists not in its being one of a sequence of *independent referential correspondences* but in its role within the *totality* of the constructed narrative world of the parable. Hermeneutically, the parable and the allegory are quite different.

The impropriety of interpreting parables as one would interpret allegories was seen perhaps as long ago as when Calvin described multipoint allegorical interpretations as idle fooleries. Certainly since Jülicher's work this principle has become commonplace in serious parable interpretation. However, even here we need to remain cautious about the peril of generalizing, for Jesus sometimes uses allegory, sometimes uses nonallegorical parable, and sometimes moves between the two. The Jewish and rabbinic term *māshāl* (Aramaic *mathlā*) only roughly approximates the Greek word *parabolē* and embraces parable, allegory, story, riddle, proverb, example, symbol, and other related forms. In Matthew 22:1, for example, we are told that Jesus spoke in parables, and we are drawn at first into a narrative about a king who gave a wedding banquet for his son and was dismayed when his guests declined their invitations. However, the story continues: "The king was angry, and he sent his troops and destroyed those murderers and burned their city" (22:7). It is difficult to see how this sentence could function as a coherent element within the single narrative perspective of the wedding parable, and it is pointless to try to ask whether declining the invitation could merit such severe military reprisals. The point is, rather, that the existence of a tradition of understanding the eschatological kingdom as a festal banquet to which disobedient Israel refused to come triggers a second-level interpretation—the destruction of Jerusalem—before the narrative comes to its close.

This reveals how closely questions about genre, subgenre, and mixed genre are bound up with an understanding of the situation common to the speaker and first readers. Without some understanding of the interpretive situation of the parable, the modern interpreter may be tempted simply to spend time fruitlessly puzzling over why the declining of an invitation leads to the burning of a whole city, or might suggest that the internal coherence of the narrative world of a parable is in general unimportant. In either case it becomes apparent that what we are to do when we interpret a parable depends on a number of specific questions about the particularities of the text, including (in many cases) its setting and its audience. It would be a mistake to argue that such questions needlessly complicate the process of interpretation. Abstract, context-free approaches do not solve these problems; they merely sweep them under the carpet. They seduce the unwary reader or the interpretive community to approach all parables—or all texts—with the same horizon of expectation and leave those which are at odds with the *a priori* model to take care of themselves as residual "problem" passages.

Similar difficulties have been the result in almost every historical period of parable interpretation whenever interpreters have tended to work with generalizing hermeneutical models. As we shall see, most patristic writers tended to adopt an interpretive procedure which made the parables primarily a support for church doctrine already derived largely from other biblical texts. Irenaeus was perhaps theologically correct when he preached on God's successive calls to his people through creation, through the Abrahamic covenant, through the ministry of Christ, and through the present preaching of the church. But it is questionable whether that represents the "meaning" of the parable of the laborers in the vineyard with general reference to their successive calls to employment. Irenaeus assumes that the meaning of the parable is generated by the sequence of referential correspondences between the two levels of what would then constitute an allegory. But to find the meaning in such a way results in the internal coherence of the narrative world *as* a single narrative being prematurely broken up in such a way that it no longer functions as a single whole. Meanwhile, the rules of faith of the patristic church become the indispensable hermeneutical key for this parable.

In spite of the criticisms made against gnostic exegesis by Irenaeus and other church fathers, one major reason for the patristic concern over an appropriate hermeneutical framework lay in the use made by the gnostics of a rival theological framework. An instructive example may be found in the interpretation of the parable of the lost sheep found in the gnostic Gospel of Truth. In Luke 15:4-7 the shepherd leaves the ninety-nine to seek the one lost sheep, and the emphasis falls on the joy of receiving the lost, in contrast to the grumblings of Jesus' pharisaic critics (15:1, 2; cf. v. 7). In the Gospel of Truth, however, the restoration of the one which changes the ninety-nine to one hundred is related to the custom of reckoning the hundred figure on the right hand, while the ninety-nine figure represents the highest possible calculation which can be indicated by gestures of the left hand and left fingers. The completion of the hundred thus supposedly points to the truth of a major gnostic doctrine: that the God of perfection is the antithesis of finitude, imperfection, or lack (represented by the left hand). The ninety-nine may be correlated with Sophia's falling into precosmic error, the wandering sheep represent the wandering planets (Greek *planē*), and Jesus stands for the filling up of the lack. The Gospel of Truth offers this "exposition": "The shepherd left behind him the ninety-nine sheep who had not strayed. He went and sought after the one which had strayed. He rejoiced when he found it. For the 'ninety-nine' is a sum [reckoned] on the left hand, which holds it. But at the time when the 'one' shall be found, the entire sum is wont to change over to the right. As that which lacks the one . . . takes it from the left side and transfers it to the right, so the sum makes one hundred, the sign of Him who is in their [i.e., the hands'] language, 'This means the Father' " (Gospel of Truth 32:1-17).[10]

Compared with this kind of hermeneutical practice, it is not surprising that the church fathers saw orthodox exegesis as more sober and less arbitrary; nor is it strange that they were quick to note the radical extent to which some prior theological framework might determine how the text was understood. The easiest guideline was simply to insist that exegesis should be tested against the rule of the doctrinal tradition of the church. The price the church paid for this, however, was a leveling of the parables to a doctrinal tool used for a purpose quite at odds with their original hermeneutical function in the ministry of Jesus.

It might be thought that the rise of modern biblical scholarship would bring with it a more liberating pluriformity in its handling of the parables. In this respect the foundational work of Adolf Jülicher did indeed observe that the Gospels contained different types of parabolic material. But such was Jülicher's *theological* insistence on the single uniform purpose of Jesus to teach general truths that he could not treat as authentic any material which seemed to reflect a more subtle, or simply different, purpose. All parables genuinely spoken by Jesus, he assumed, were similes, not metaphors, and were clear, not puzzling. In effect they all articulated general truths in a manner which made them self-explanatory. Admittedly Jülicher divided his broad category of *eigentliche Rede*,[11] or simile in contrast to metaphor, into at least three subcategories: the similitude *(Gleichnis)* compares sentences or thoughts; the parable proper *(Parabel)* unfolds an imagined story; while example stories *(Beispielerzählung)* draw points of comparison between characters in the story and the reader.[12] Nevertheless, the *hermeneutical* function remains broadly the same. It is largely didactic, cognitive, cerebral, and direct.

The parable of the dishonest manager (Luke 16:1-8), for example, in Jülicher's approach is simply a tale with the general moral that wise use of the present is the condition of a happy future.[13] The parable of the talents tells the reader that a reward is earned only by performance.[14] Jülicher had rightly expelled allegorical interpretation from places where it did not belong. But he had also expelled it from where it did belong, and more to the point had been no more successful in avoiding some generalizing hermeneutical principle than the earlier generations against which he was reacting. Jülicher's hermeneutics reflects his own horizon of expectation concerning the method and message of Jesus, and in this respect it controls the text more decisively than the text controls the hermeneutics.

We need not trace this pattern through the entire history of parable interpretation. We should note that in general there has been a steady trend in the direction of allowing hermeneutical theory to be shaped by the particularities of the text. Even so, some approaches which seem at first sight to do justice to this point turn out to be less innocent than they appear. Those approaches, for example, which emphasize the polyvalency of meaning often carry with them some overarching theory about hermeneutical function, such as the supposed subversion of the hearer's world. J. D. Crossan writes, "Myth establishes world . . . satire attacks world. Parable subverts world."[15] But if parable *always* subverts world, does this mean that it subverts, on a second reading, the new world of Jesus' world for which it has already made space, or alternatively that the parable can say nothing to one whose world has already been subverted? Clearly this is bound up with questions about tradition, about so-called insiders and outsiders, and about audience criticism. The problem is not that the hermeneutical theorist should refrain from offering general hermeneutical *models*. Crossan's work is in this respect fruitful and very constructive. The problem is, rather, that such models are sometimes treated as overarching interpretive keys rather than as exploratory or functional working models. The search for models which reveal resonances or parallels between the hermeneutical functions of different texts remains a fundamental and indispensable part of hermeneutics. Without such a search hermeneutics would fall back into exegesis. But questions about the scope and application of competing or complementary models cannot be answered in abstract terms alone.

One reason why this is so, quite apart from related questions about genre and situation, arises from Jesus' own words about the purpose of parabolic speech in Mark 4:10-12 and its parallel in Matthew.[13] As P. S. Hawkins recently noted, "The difficult truth about parable[s]" (i.e., those which resist some easy hermeneutical formula) is "the fact that they are the *utterance but not the unveiling* of what has been hidden; a proclamation of mystery rather than an explanation of it."[16] This point both illuminates and relativizes the now standard distinction between parable and allegory. As Hans-Josef Klauck and others have shown, we do not do justice to the parables by using the kind of allegorical interpretation which presupposes some general key as a decoding device.[17] But the Gospel parables may and do include allegory in the form of extended metaphors which demand perception, engagement, and interpretation on the part of the audience. Madeleine Boucher rightly comments, "The charge . . . that Mark distorted the parable as a verbal construct is simply unfounded. Mark has not taken clear, straightforward speech, the parable, and transformed it into obscure esoteric speech, the allegory. He has rather taken . . . the double-meaning effect, and made it the starting-point of a theological theme concerning the audience's resistance to hearing the word." "The parables," she continues, "convey not secret information, but the requirements made of the hearer. . . . Those who do not understand are those who will not allow its lesson to impinge on their own existence."[18]

Audience Criticism and Reader-response Hermeneutics

If the parables of Jesus demand from the reader a readiness to respond, naturally the biblical interpreter will want to explore the model of reader-response hermeneutics in literary theory. Significantly, the place of the reader or audience in the interpretive process has been stressed in three quite distinct ways in three different movements of thought: in biblical studies, in literary and aesthetic theory, and in philosophical hermeneutics.

At the outset we should stress that the movement known in biblical studies as audience criticism is very different in both concern and perspective from reader-response theory in literary studies and aesthetics. But this very difference makes it even more necessary to compare the two movements for their respective strengths and weaknesses for biblical interpretation.

Audience criticism in biblical studies of the Gospels is notably represented in J. Arthur Baird's *Audience Criticism and the Historical Jesus.*[19] Baird begins by pointing out that Jesus was a selective teacher. Jesus spoke in parables "as they were able to hear it," but "privately to his disciples he explained everything" (Mark 4:33, 34); "not all men can receive the precept but only those to whom it is given" (Matthew 19:11). But the Evangelists were no less concerned than Jesus about the audience and audience identification. As Baird points out, of the 422 units of the Huck-Lietzmann synopsis of the first three Gospels, the audience is clearly designated in 395, or 94 percent. Broad audience identifications differentiate the twelve disciples; the larger "crowd" of disciples, or "those who were with the Twelve"; the opponent crowd; and the opponents themselves. Each group, however, includes further subcategories: the opponents, for example, include Pharisees, scribes, lawyers, the high priests, elders, and the sanhedrin. In this opponent group Baird examines seventeen subcategories represented by corresponding Greek words or phrases.[20] Baird further considers the use of audience criticism as a tool of inquiry to investigate the relations between specific audience identifications and sources, forms, and redactions. This last exercise entails meticulous statistical examinations which draw on computer data and a very close knowledge of the text. With respect to the parables this leads to such specific questions as that of the correlations between types of metaphorical imagery and types of audience.[21]

Three conclusions, among others, emerge from Baird's careful work. First Baird shows by his uncovering of certain irregularities and patterned correlations in the text itself that many *logia* which have been attributed by a number of scholars to the early church or to redactional activity do go back to Jesus himself. Baird reaches a more positive verdict both about the historicity of the *logia* and about the genuineness of their audience settings than most of his predecessors.

Second, his work in effect reiterates the point that what constitutes explication, interpretation, or understanding of the parables depends partly on questions about audience. What "making clear" consists of depends on the question "clear *to whom?*" Because the parables entail at least four kinds of audience, there seem to be at least four ways of understanding the meaning of the parable. Baird terms these "semi-allegorical," "thematic," "contextual," and "internal."[22]

Third, and most important for this stage of the present discussion, Baird expounds audience criticism "as a hermeneutical tool." He declares, "The audience was of great importance to those who recorded the tradition because they believed the message of the *logia* itself was audience-centered." Jesus accommodated his message to his audience "to such a degree that the nature of the audience became an important part of the message of the *logion* itself. This was then preserved with unique fidelity for . . . the audience was needed for the correct and meaningful reproduction of his teaching. This means to us that the audience has become a hermeneutical factor of first importance. It means that we cannot really understand what the *logia* are saying until we understand the audience to which they are attributed."[23]

The originality and importance of Baird's work on the Gospels has received less attention than it deserves. Only K. L. Schmidt and T. W. Manson seem to have studied with adequate seriousness, before Baird, the role of audiences in the Gospels, even though in the area of the New Testament Epistles the hermeneutical significance of the audience has long been recognized as being of primary importance. It has long been taken for granted that questions about Paul's readers and the Pauline churches shed important light on both the meaning and the relevance of his words.[24] A recent study by Robert Jewett applies audience criticism to the non-Pauline Epistle to the Hebrews.[25] However, Baird's work represents a turning point for work on the Gospels, especially on the parables. The hermeneutical significance of the audience criticism movement can be seen not only in its concern about situational particularity but also in two equally important directions: first, the participatory dimension of reader-response; and second, the need for answering questions about application or relevance with at least some reference to whether there is any correspondence between the situation of the audience to whom the text was first directed and that of the reader to whom it is directed today.

The second movement to be considered is the application of reader-response hermeneutics in literary theory. In some respects it parallels audience criticism in biblical studies insofar as both movements pay attention to the reader's status and situation, but it is much more radical and much less controlled in its conclusions. Responsible interpretation in audience criticism depends on a rough correspondence between the situation of the original addressees of the text and that of a modern reader or interpretive community. By contrast, it is far more difficult to stipulate the limits of interpretive responsibility in the case of a radical version of reader-response theory.

Already within the last few years reader-response theory has entered New Testament studies as an interpretive tool. The work of Robert Fowler on the feeding miracles in Mark (1981) and that of R. Alan Culpepper on the literary design of the Fourth Gospel (1983) provide two examples.[26] Fowler builds partly upon the approach of Wayne Booth in his books *The Rhetoric of Fiction* and *A Rhetoric of Irony*. The Gospel of Mark, Fowler argues, is written in such a way as to take account of expectations on the part of the reader which the Markan text may subsequently confirm, fulfill, frustrate, or revise. This explains why Mark drops certain clues in otherwise surprising places which encourage certain attitudes concerning Jesus. In particular Fowler sees this concern to utilize, even to manipulate, reader expectations as the key to the so-called doublet about two feedings of the multitudes in Mark 6:30-44 and in 8:1-10.[27] Mark, he believes, includes his own Markan account of the feeding of the five thousand before the traditional material about the feeding of the four thousand two chapters later in order to point up the unbelief of the disciples' question in 8:4: "How can one feed these men with bread here in the desert?" Mark, he believes, is concerned not simply to narrate a miracle, but to produce a particular active *perception* of its significance on the part of the reader. The *prima facie* absurdity of the disciples asking how Jesus could feed four thousand people, when two chapters earlier he has already fed five thousand, provides the conditions for what Wayne Booth had called "intended irony." The intended or implied *reader's* expectation is consciously, and sharply, at variance with that of the disciples, and the disciples' view of Jesus is consciously transcended by the reader at this point.

Fowler's work thus utilizes in the service of Markan studies some of the standard tools of reader-response theory, in which attention is paid to the roles, expectations, and attitudes of the implied reader envisioned by the author. Culpepper applies these working tools to the Gospel of John, drawing distinctions (borrowed from Iser and others) between (1) John's actual readers; (2) John's authorial audience; (3) a narrative audience who accepted the story on its own terms; and (4) his ideal narrative reader. This ideal reader accepts John's own judgments and appreciates his irony in such a way as to move toward fresh appreciations through the Gospel's story and symbolism. The Johannine narrative, he concludes, operates retrospectively, telling a story that is a blend of historical tradition and faith. The Gospel narrative, in sum, "draws together the reader and the author, readers and Jesus, this world and the world above."[28]

Culpepper's work builds on that of Wolfgang Iser among others no less explicitly than Fowler's has built on that of Iser and Wayne Booth. But in literary theory the term "reader-response" may sometimes denote a wide range of perspectives and approaches. At one end of the spectrum there is a general emphasis on the reader which may be broader and less specific than that of Booth and of Iser, while at the other end of the spectrum appears an approach which is far more radical in its hermeneutical implications. Probably the most radical exponent of reader-response hermeneutics is Stanley Fish.[29]

However, it is also possible, though perhaps less helpful, to use the term "reader-response" in a much looser sense to indicate a broad group of writers who share a general concern to move hermeneutic emphasis away from the authors of texts to the readers of texts. Such a tendency is apparent in works as diverse as Foucault's essay "What Is an Author?" Roland Barthes's "From Work to Text," and many of the writings of Jacques Derrida.[30] We might also distinguish as distinctive positions within this broad emphasis Todorov's stress on reading or construction and Maranda's work on how the reader uses the text to come to terms with his or her own world in a variety of theoretical and practical ways.[31]

Meaning, for most of these writers, is always potential in terms of the text, but actual in relation to the reader. No meaning is already "there" in a text, or at least "there" in some objectivist sense, apart from a horizon of expectations brought to a text by the reader. As a suggestive aphorism by Fish asserts, "the reader's response is not *to* the meaning; it *is* the meaning."[32] Fish traces the story of his own intellectual pilgrimage since 1970 by describing how his earlier doubts about the autonomy of the text gave way gradually to a much more radical appreciation of the decisive role played by the reader not only in the process of understanding and interpretation but even in the birth of meaning.

This process began, for Fish, with an appreciation of the temporal dimension in which the potential meanings made possible by the text are actualized only in a process of readings. The spatial form of the text provides a less important key to the nature of its meaning than its temporal appropriation in a series of concrete interactions with the expectations and projections of its readers. The question "What does this mean?" came to be replaced by a second: "What does this do?" This led, secondly, to an investigation of the part played by interpretive communities: how their very expectations concerning what might *count* as meaning were inseparable from their assumptions or even conclusions about what kind of meaning *lay*, as it were, already in the text. Later still, Fish perceived that this position was, in a sense, self-defeating. He comments, "I did what critics always do: I 'saw' what my interpretive principles permitted or directed me to see, and then I turned around and attributed what I had 'seen' to a text and an intention. What my principles direct me to 'see' are readers performing acts."[33] Units of sense generated by the text "do not lie innocently in the world; rather, they are themselves constituted by an interpretive act. The facts one points to are still there (in a sense that would not be consoling to an objectivist) but only as a consequence of the interpretive (man-made) model that has called them into being."[34]

Fish's most recent conclusion, then, expressed negatively, is that a text does not generate determinate meaning "independently of social and institutional circumstances."[35] The reader and the reader's social-ethical-intellectual community contribute decisively to the final meaning of the text. Once again we may repeat that not all writers who are concerned with audience response go as far as Stanley Fish. Susan Suilleman significantly entitles an essay which introduces this subject "Varieties of Audience-Oriented Criticism."[36]

The third parallel movement is the application of similar principles in systematic and philosophical theology combined to emphasize the interpreting subject and the importance of his or her preunderstanding in the act or process of communication. Although in one sense the major turn in hermeneutics took place with Schleiermacher and Dilthey, James Robinson has good grounds for calling attention to the far-reaching effects of Karl Barth's commentary on Romans. Barth's fundamental methodological claim was that the objectivism of liberal scholarship represented by Jülicher and by Harnack could not as a matter of principle do justice to the biblical text.[37] This methodological claim was effectively strengthened for theology by the common ground which it shared with Rudolf Bultmann's emphasis on the kerygmatic nature of the New Testament. The New Testament, Bultmann urged, did not convey timeless information unrelated to situations and to hearers, but addressed the hearer with a practical message which demanded practical response. But if this is so, he urged, the preliminary questions or expectations with which the reader approaches the text decisively shape what he or she will "find" there.

In the era following Barth and Bultmann, Ernst Fuchs in Germany, Gerhard Ebeling in Switzerland, and Robert Funk and others in America developed individual perspectives which underlined this concern with the role of the reader.[38] Out of this work emerged the generally accepted notion that communication and interpretation were to be seen as *events* or *processes,* rather than merely the expression of ideas, and that this way of viewing interpretation was suggested by two quite distinct philosophical traditions. On the one hand, it emerged from the philosophies of Heidegger and Gadamer; on the other hand it was suggested, even if less directly, by the work of Wittgenstein, Austin, and speech-act theorists such as J. R. Searle. Hermeneutics came to be seen as the operative engagement or interaction between the horizon of the text and the horizon of the reader. The problem of hermeneutics was the problem of two horizons, and because of my earlier work under this title I need pursue questions about this third movement no further at this point.[39]

This sketch of three very different audience-oriented movements in hermeneutics does not constitute a defense of them. Whether these approaches result in gain or whether they risk distinct loss will become apparent not simply when we theorize in the abstract, but when we attempt to test their adequacy in the light of case studies— such as our specific inquiries about the parables of Jesus.

The Need for a Reader-response Approach to the Parables

By contrast with recent developments in parable interpretation during the last decade, the work of Jülicher tends to reduce the role of the reader to a bare minimum. But the reason for this can easily be mistaken. The problem is not primarily that Jülicher's "one-point" approach oversimplifies the parables, although this does occur in some instances. The difficulty is rather that, as Robert Funk has more than once stated, "the parables were understood [by Jülicher] as example stories or as illustrations of a point that could have been made, without essential loss, in discursive, non-figurative language."[40] The parables tend to function, in Jülicher's work, as broad, easily assimilated truths which can be too neatly packaged as a bundle of cognitive concepts.

In all fairness to Jülicher, we ought not perhaps to accept without qualification the verdict of A. M. Hunter and others that his interpretations of the parables reduce them to nothing more than prudential platitudes. But Jülicher certainly moves too far in this direction, and he does so repeatedly. For example when he carefully examines in considerable detail the three seed parables in Mark 4 (the sower, 4:3-8; the seed growing of itself, 4:26-29; and the mustard seed, 4:30-32), Jülicher insists that these convey not a merely prudential lesson about uninterrupted growth but a prophetical assurance, in the face of anxious concern, that future fulfillment of the kingdom is certain.[41] Thus the sower parable teaches that the seed of the word finds a lasting place only among those who respond to the gospel and bear fruit. The seed growing "of itself" shows that the certainty of the kingdom's reaching its purpose does not depend on human capacities for good or evil. The mustard seed suggests that we cannot tell the nature of the end simply by looking at the apparent insignificance of the beginning.[42] Certainly this is not, as is sometimes claimed, mere nineteenth-century liberal theology; Jülicher's attention to exegetical detail takes him beyond this. Nevertheless, there is neither the challenge nor the offense nor the transformation of values which makes heavy demands on the reader and which historically actually led Jesus to the cross. The telltale phrase Jülicher uses is that the interpreter can easily sum up the chief thoughts of these parables—and these "chief thoughts" prove in the end to be not very contestable.[43]

In one sense Jülicher was not wrong to stress the cognitive content of the parables. Later interpreters need to see in the parables a body of material which can be described conceptually in order to abstract and retrospectively define their content. Biblical research has shown that while it is useful to draw a working distinction between preaching *(kerygma)* and teaching *(didachē)* this distinction is not absolute. Indeed preaching includes information about states of affairs. But Jülicher's mistake lay in his preoccupation with this aspect, as if cognitive abstraction was the primary or even sole hermeneutical goal and as if meaning were reducible to conceptual content alone, in isolation from problems about function, preunderstanding, temporality, and recontextualization. In any case, very many of Jülicher's interpretations are even broader, more general, and more abstract than those we have cited by way of example. For instance, after some twenty-five pages of discussion of the rich man and Lazarus (Luke 16:19-31) he interprets the story as passing on the lesson of "joy in a life of suffering and fear at a life of enjoyment."[44] There is an unmistakable flattening reductionism in "thoughts" which invite only fairly easy assent.

C. H. Dodd moved further in the direction of reader-response theory when he insisted that the parable "arrests the hearer by its vividness or strangeness . . . leaving the mind in sufficient doubt about its precise application to tease it into active thought."[45] Funk rightly comments, "The parable is not closed, so to speak, until the listener is drawn into it as participant. The application is not specified until the hearer, led by the 'logic' of the parable, specifies it for himself."[46] Dodd's exposition of the parable of the dishonest manager (Luke 16:1-13) as a parable of crisis illustrates this principle.[47] We miss the point if we debate the ethics of the rogue who, threatened with dismissal, set up questionable deals with the owner's creditors so that they would see that he would not suffer when he lost his job. Why does the master (whether *ho kurios* means the employer or Jesus) "commend" the manager who has just reduced the amounts owed by his employer's debtors? The reader wrestles with the message on two levels. First, it appears that at least the dishonest manager may be commended for being a shrewd fellow who knows how to serve his own interests when he is up against a crisis. Second, it becomes clear at the level of *kerygma* that the crisis provoked by the coming of Jesus also, and no less, demands the kind of urgent action which makes all other considerations subordinate ones.

The major problem left by Dodd's interpretation concerns the status of the so-called editorial conclusions. Do verses 8b-12 actually undermine the hermeneutical function of this parable as Jesus told it? I have tried to come to terms with this difficult exegetical problem in an earlier article on this subject.[48] The major point, however, remains that even when certain specific maxims are placed at the end of the parable, there remains an element of open-endedness or ambiguity which can be resolved only when the hearer or reader actively wrestles with the text. The reader has to put two and two together unassisted by a third party's key to interpretation; if someone else supplies the "answer," it is no longer the same discovery.

Even for Dodd, however, this process of interpretation remains primarily one of conscious cognitive operation. He stresses situation, kerygma, and response, but praxis seems to be a second step which follows *after* cognitive reflection. Dodd's approach fits in with Hirsch's distinction between meaning and significance, but it does not quite do justice to the subtle relation between the two. Joachim Jeremias builds on, develops, and modifies Dodd's approach. Using form-critical tools, Jeremias sees the parables as *announcements*. He declares, "One thing above all becomes evident: it is that all the parables of Jesus compel his hearers to come to a decision about his person and mission."[49] Jeremias's work is rightly regarded as a major classic of modern biblical studies, and it will remain a standard work. The sixth German edition of 1962 also took account of the then-discovered Gospel of Thomas and its possible significance for parable interpretation. Yet hermeneutically Jeremias's work is profoundly ambiguous.

On the surface Jeremias repeatedly puts forward the claim that the hermeneutical function of the parables is to compel *decision*. Yet, as Norman Perrin points out, the major concern of Jeremias's book is to view the parables as "sources" for a reconstruction of the content of the *message* of Jesus of Nazareth.[50] Although *kerygma* and *didachē* are never equated with each other, the world "message" or "announcement" is sometimes replaced by "instruction." The message of the parables becomes an exposition of "themes" of instruction. For example, "Now is the day of salvation" becomes "a threat or cry of warning . . . to illustrate his [Jesus'] instruction."[51] All of Jesus' parables can in Jeremias's view be classified under eight broad themes: the day of salvation; God's mercy for sinners—the great assurance; the imminence of catastrophe; it may be too late; the challenge of the hour; realized discipleship; the via dolorosa; and the consummation. This aspect of Jeremias's work has evoked the most criticism from more recent hermeneutical approaches. Perrin calls these themes "rubrics" and comments: "Whereas a summary of Jülicher's general moral principles looks very much like a manifesto of nineteenth-century theological liberalism, this list of rubrics [i.e., Jeremias's themes] looks very much like a summary of a rather conservative Lutheran piety. But . . . what is important is that the very nature of the parables of Jesus as texts forbids the reduction of his message to a series of general moral principles or to a set of rubrics. Parables as parables do not have a 'message,' they tease the mind into ever new perceptions of reality.''[52] With an implied allusion to Paul Ricoeur, Perrin adds: "They function like symbols in that they 'give rise to thought.' ''[53]

The accuracy of Perrin's comments about the hermeneutical function of parables need not be decided at this point, although we shall argue that they set up an unnecessary polarization between message and reader-orientation. The approach of Jeremias, however, admittedly focuses too narrowly on one aspect of interpretation because he allows his methodological goal of using the parables in the service of a historical reconstruction of the message of the Jesus of history to occupy too central a place as a hermeneutical model. Jeremias allows the ambiguity between an emphasis on thematic truths and reader-decision to arise because he fails to see the full consequences of the action model of parabolic language to which his constructive emphasis on language intention almost brings him. He is correct in seeing the parables of Jesus as, in effect, speech-acts; that is, they attack, they rebuke, they claim, they defend. They are *acts* of utterance produced in situations of conflict and tension. But by allowing a concern for historical reconstruction to dominate his hermeneutical work, Jeremias allows this functional perspective, this action model, to slip from view as he gives more and more emphasis to a process of retrospective abstraction which reduces the parables to components of an overall message. This produces, in turn, a further problem, for now the cognitive content of the message of Jesus himself comes to be regarded as different in form and content from the subject matter which emerges when the post-Easter community recontextualizes the parables.[54] The "authentic" parables of Jesus are expanded, interpreted, and recontextualized by the Evangelists and the early community through such processes as translocation, changes of audience, allegorization, and the addition of hortatory and moralizing conclusions. A radical reader-response approach, such as we find in Stanley Fish, would claim that these acts of recontextualization on the part of successive layers of readers do in practice *constitute* the meaning of the parables. But since Jeremias's concern is to attempt "to recover the original significance of the parables," the status of their interpretation by the Evangelists remains unclear.[55]

Jeremias's work left a hermeneutical vacuum which a number of recent writers have hastened to fill. The problem is that in their enthusiasm to explore the role of the reader many have assumed that the inadequacies of Jeremias's work arose from his having a historical rather than a literary concern, as if somehow an interpreter could not—or should not—combine both concerns. The model of speech-act-in-situation has been effectively ignored, and a concern with history or situation increasingly neglected. The unspoken assumption seems to be that a historically serious hermeneutic cannot do full justice to the role of the modern reader. Thus the promise held out by Baird and audience criticism is ignored in the rush to cash in on "literary" approaches.

The most recent of those who have polarized the history-versus-literature perspectives is John Sider in his current article "Rediscovering the Parables: The Logic of the Jeremias Tradition."[56] In his first section, entitled Literature vs History? he exploits the notion that to heed the lessons offered by literary critics such as Helen Gardiner, C. S. Lewis, or Northrop Frye is thereby to reject the importance of historical inquiry. But there are at least two confusions which run through this article. First, some perfectly valid and forceful criticisms of Jeremias's specific historical judgments are treated as if they were grounds for dismissing historical inquiry even of a more careful and judicious kind. Second, Sider confuses the kind of historical inquiry which uses texts merely as tools for the reconstruction of ideas or events by the religious historian with the kind of historical inquiry which proceeds in order to do full justice to the texts themselves.[57]

In an attempt to move forward more constructively it is necessary to take at least the following five steps: (1) to appreciate the positive and indispensable nature of historical inquiry; (2) to become aware of its limitations; (3) to appreciate the positive and constructive gains of reader-response hermeneutics and literary theory; (4) to become aware of their one-sidedness and inadequacy as general hermeneutical theories; and (5) to explore what hermeneutical models might allow us to hold together all that has been learned from these first four steps. While no single hermeneutical model holds the key to all problems, this present discussion urges the view that an action model moves the discussion forward more constructively than most other models. Action-theory models bring into focus the multilevel functions of speech-acts without committing us to the anarchy of radically polyvalent meaning. A speech-act, or series of speech-acts, may be able simultaneously to project narrative-worlds *and* assert states of affairs *and* transform the perceptions of readers. At the same time, certain fundamental distinctions remain in force. In Wolterstorff's words, an action model allows us to "distinguish clearly between the action of fictionally *projecting* a world, on the one hand, and the action of *describing* the contents of an already projected world, on the other" (my italics).[58] Jeremias is too eager to move from a speech-act (e.g., attacking pharisaic assumptions) to the content of a projected world (e.g., the message of God's mercy for sinners). As his critics see, Jeremias overlooks other dimensions and effects of the speech-act. As Wolterstorff observes: "By performing one and another action . . . the artist generates a variety of other, distinct, actions."[59] But this does not mean, as some of Jeremias's critics fail to see, that the situation of the speech-act surrenders its role as a control over what reader-acts might now be considered as *appropriate* or *responsible* acts.

The Problems and Inadequacy of a
Reader-response Approach to the Parables

Four major New Testament scholars paved the way for a reader-response approach to the parables: Ernst Fuchs, Robert Funk, Dan Otto Via, and John Dominic Crossan.[60] Their foundational work has also moved discussion forward in two related areas. Hans Weder, Sallie (TeSelle) McFague, and Hans-Josef Klauck[61] have further explored the relation between parable and metaphor; Susan Wittig, Mary Tolbert, and others have developed the debate in relation to semiotics.[62] We might instructively examine, if only briefly, one or two examples of this work.

Crossan takes up the notion of a projected "world." This category finds its place in parable studies in the first place not so much from literary theory as from the thought of Martin Heidegger as mediated through Ernst Fuchs. A parable projects a world which is at first familiar to the hearer, in which the hearer is at home. Narrative, together with metaphor, draws the hearer in as participant rather than as spectator. Metaphor is neither a merely explanatory nor ornamental device, but that which draws the hearers into "seeing" a new possibility. But when metaphor is extended into a metaphorical narrative, the initial invitation to enter a familiar "world" may not be as innocent as it at first seems. As the reader is enthralled and drawn along, he or she arrives at the place where a further action occurs: an act which surprises, or reverses, the reader's prior expectations. The parable world diverges so drastically from the reader's own that it constitutes a challenge, and the reader has to go along with it or reject it. However, perceptual and pragmatic dimensions are intertwined. The parable world projects a perspective which the reader otherwise might not have been able to grasp.

Crossan's interpretation of the parable of the good Samaritan (Luke 10:30-37) provides a concrete example. He insists, "the point is not that one should help the neighbor in need."[63] If so, Jesus might better have made the wounded man a Samaritan and the helper a lay Jew representative of Jesus' audience. Since Jews "have no dealings with Samaritans" (John 4:9), the story challenges the hearer "to put together two impossible and contradictory words for the same person: 'Samaritan' (10:33) and 'neighbor' (10:36)."[64] The parable's *action* at the deepest level is to overthrow or to subject the hearer's preconceived notions about goodness and evil, to make room for an experience and understanding of divine grace. Such an interpretation does not conflict, however (as Crossan thinks it does), with the lawyer's question and reply in the Lukan frame. The question in verse 37b puts the lawyer's horizon of expectations in question not only by relativizing his prior notions of good and evil but also by placing him alongside the Samaritan. The action of the parable involves both the transformation of his perceptions and the transformation of his practical attitudes. What it is *not* is simply a moralizing tale; *nor* is it an allegory of the incarnation. What it *is* entails a reader-response.

Crossan's positive emphasis on reader-response has its drawbacks, which we will turn to shortly. We should first, however, examine Susan Wittig's use of semiotic theory to explore the reader-response approach. She begins her study by asking the question: how is it that a text can be plurisignificant, or polyvalent? She offers two answers. One source of polyvalency is the differences of purposes, goals, and methods that the interpreter brings to the text. A second source is the multiplicity of ways in which the reader may "complete" the meaning of the text. She defines a parable, from a semiotic viewpoint, as "a duplex connotative system in which the precise significance is left unstated."[65] At the level of the narrative world alone, a linguistic signifier (e.g., "a certain man had two sons," Luke 15:11) denotes a referent such as an object or event, real or fictional (e.g., the father and the two sons in the story world). But this entire unit of first-order signifier and signified, Wittig suggests, now functions as a second-order signifier to designate some unstated signified which can only be a psychological construct supplied by the hearer. Whereas the first-order signifier and signified are linked by linguistic convention, no social system of linguistic conventions forms the basis upon which the hearer constructs the signified at the second level: "The second-order signifier . . . is linked iconically to its unstated, implicit signified."[66] The hearer must make the link; the purpose of the parable is to allow him or her to do this: "The final signified remains unstated, giving to the system a dynamic unstable *indeterminacy* which invites, even compels, the perceiver to complete the signification."[67]

Those familiar with reader-response theory in literary studies will recognize the influence of Wolfgang Iser at this point. However, Wittig's work reveals some practical strengths and weaknesses in its application as a hermeneutical model to parable interpretation. The strength of this approach is the role accorded to the hearer or the reader of a kind which has been neglected in the work of Jülicher and Jeremias. The difficulties, however, cluster around three distinct issues. First, the work of Crossan on the parables and on polyvalent meaning leads explicitly to the kind of hermeneutical radicalism and theoretical skepticism that characterize the work of Jacques Derrida and Richard Rorty. This in turn throws into relief some of the theoretical problems which beset the work of Stanley Fish. Second, at a more pragmatic level the actual interpretations of parables suggested by those who expound this approach repeatedly demonstrate its unsatisfactory nature. Is Mary Tolbert, for example, successful in wishing to utilize Wittig's approach while attempting to interpret parables in ways "congruent" with the text? Finally, can any theory of hermeneutics claim to be adequate when it relies entirely on *one* hermeneutical model, namely that of reader-response?

Crossan explicitly poses the first problem, that of hermeneutical radicalism, when he traces the transition from existentialism through structuralism to the poststructuralism of Derrida. The "existential nausea," he writes, was "the ontological disappointment of one who, having been taught that there is some overarching logical meaning beyond our perception, has come at length to believe that there is no such fixed center towards which our searchings strive. Existentialism is thus the dull receding roar of classicism and rationalism while structuralism is a new flood of the tide."[68] Crossan attempts to show that the increasingly conscious conviction from Nietzsche through Freud and Heidegger to Derrida reaches its climax in the metaphor of the hermeneutical labyrinth. The labyrinth has no center and is infinitely expansible since we create it by our language and interpretive perceptions as we move through it ourselves. The only appropriate response is that which takes its starting point from Johann Huizinga's *Homo Ludens* as modified and developed by Jacques Ehrmann. It is a process of "free activity" in an orderly manner in the course of which " 'All reality is caught up in the play of the concepts which designate it.' . . . A megametaphor, . . . the play of semiosis."[69] Polyvalency of meaning and interpretation is inevitable, for everything exists within signs and even the distinction between signifier and signified dissolves. If anything is "reality," it is what we experience in the play of semiosis.

Parables function in this semiotic context to break images, to challenge fixed assumptions, and to carry us forward in the only way that can handle the ultimate paradox of hermeneutics: how can we think of anything *as* anything if we are still making up our minds what to think of it *as?* Parables subvert, relativize, and re-relativize each and every reading. "The game can be played repeatedly and continuously. So also with the play of interpretation on ludic allegory in parable. Since you cannot interpret absolutely, you interpret forever. This paradox . . . precludes any final or canonical interpretation. . . . Positively, it turns the story outward as a metaphor for its own very process of interpretation. This is polyvalent narration or ludic allegory at its deepest level."[70]

Crossan comes very close here philosophically to Richard Rorty. Rorty writes, "Hermeneutics is not 'another way of knowing'— 'understanding' as opposed to 'explanation.' It is better seen as another way of coping."[71] Radical hermeneutics is simply a way of responding to the acknowledged relativity of all interpretation by choosing practice rather than theory. The text is no more and no less than what the reader makes it. In literary theory this is close to the position of Stanley Fish. Fish spells out this position with delightful and disarming honesty in the giveaway title of the introduction to his recent book: "How I Stopped Worrying and Learned to Love Interpretation."[72] A thinker can "stop worrying" only when either of two events occurs: (1) when he finds the solution to all the serious problems that face him; *or* (2) when he endures the tension of these problems no longer and is driven to the belief that one side of the tension rests on an illusion. Then he can without bad conscience simply cut the knots on the ground that the problem was never genuine in the first place.

Hermeneutics cuts through interpretive knots by one of two opposite claims: either (1) the claim that the text has some *inherent, internal, or "obvious"* meaning apart from the stance and expectations of the interpreter; or (2) the claim that the text has *no* meaning apart from the stance and expectations of the interpreter. The first view represents a kind of objectivism that is at odds with the whole discipline of hermeneutics; the second view reduces hermeneutics to radical relativism and skepticism. Fish throws all his weight behind the view that the meaning of a text *seems* "inescapable" only when the reader brings some prestructured understanding to the text.[73] The title *Is There a Text in This Class?* illustrates this claim. From within one horizon of expectation it means quite "obviously": " Does this class have a set text?" From within a different horizon of expectation it "obviously" means: "Is this class conducted on the assumption that a text has a givenness and stability which is more than merely a reader's response?" Stanley Fish can "stop worrying" only by entirely subordinating the givenness of the horizon of the text to the horizon of the reader. But this is not a *solution,* it is merely a *decision;* and given the standpoint of Rorty, Crossan, Derrida, and others it cannot be defended by granting it any other status. In Derrida, truth has virtually become merely autobiography.

We come, then, to the second major criticism. What, in practice, has been the outcome of applying this approach to the parables? We might easily cite irresponsible and unscholarly examples of this approach, but this would not constitute a fair assessment of the methodology. The work of Mary Ann Tolbert represents a careful and conscientious attempt to draw on the work of Crossan and Wittig while remaining faithful, as far as possible, to the text. From Fish's standpoint hers is still the work of a worrier, and to my mind is all the better for that. Tolbert repeatedly asserts that "the interpretation must 'fit' the parable story. Further, it must deal with the entire configuration of the story and not just one part of it."[74] At the same time, on the basis of Susan Wittig's reader-response approach, "There is no one correct interpretation of a parable, though there may be limits of congruency that invalidate some readings."[75]

Some actual examples of such interpretation, however, will dismay most biblical specialists. The parable of the prodigal son, Tolbert urges, employs three characters, an adult and two "children."[76] The adult must mediate between the two children. One son has wasted himself on a dissipated life; the other son is judgmental and unforgiving. "These three elements are present in the psyche of every individual. The voice inside us which demands the fulfilling of every desire, the breaking of every taboo, is pitted against the often equally strong voice of harsh judgment on those desires. . . . Mediating between these two voices is the one who attempts to bring unity and harmony, . . . the resolution of conflicts within the psyche of every individual."[77] It is a short step for Tolbert to represent the father, the elder son, and the prodigal as, respectively, the ego, the superego, and the id of Freudian psychology. "Just as the younger son of the story embodies some of the aspects of Freud's conception of the id, the elder son exhibits striking analogies with the ego ideal or 'conscience.' The superego . . . is the seat of morality, religion, law, and judgment."[78] The father, however, is at pains to say that he needs both sons. Both sons are necessary and valued elements of the family. The father corresponds to the Freudian ego, for "the father is both the unifying center of the parable and its most vacillating figure."[79]

At the end of this account, Tolbert points out that once the reader is in the domain of psychoanalysis, there is no reason why this account should have *automatically* privileged status over others. So she suggests a "second reading" in which other psychological categories are employed. She recognizes that these are "contextual systems," that they must be open to evaluation, and that they must be faithful to the text. While she allows these other psychological approaches as valid interpretations, in the end she decides that her first reading is more appropriate when she examines "internally" the totality of the story again in relation to her interpretation.

In effect, though, the only working criterion for valid interpretation Tolbert applies is one of general "congruence" with a text which is virtually cut loose from its situation and left open to use by a reader who is free to utilize different aspects of his or her own "contextual system." Susan Wittig also relies on the criterion of "congruency," but her admission concerning its open-endedness is more radical and explicit. She concedes, "From the sender's point of view, the receiver who arrives at a signified other than the one which was intended is 'wrong.' . . . [But] from another more objective point of view what is demonstrated here is the ability to semantically alter a sign by embedding it within another belief-system, and validating the new significance by reference to those beliefs."[80]

At this point, however, an interpretive community that regards the words of Jesus of Nazareth as privileged or authoritative cannot but feel ill at ease. Christian interpreters may even begin to regret too hastily criticizing the attention paid by Jeremias and others to the Jesus of history and the situations out of which he spoke. But this brings us back to our earlier claim about undue polarization, and also constitutes our third major criticism of the approach under discussion. Reader-response theory carries us forward constructively, especially in interpreting the parables, but it remains a *single* hermeneutical perspective which is inadequate when it is given the status of a comprehensive hermeneutical model. Neither the multidimensional character of speech-act theory nor the complexities of the process of recontextualization has been given adequate attention in these approaches. Our next task will be to examine these aspects more closely.

The Contribution of the Action Model: Toward Responsible Interpretation

At this point, two conclusions, among others, have emerged. First, reader-response hermeneutics provides a valuable way of discovering perspectives in the interpretation of the parables of Jesus; this approach received inadequate attention in traditional biblical hermeneutics and especially in the period from Jülicher to Jeremias. Second, reader-response hermeneutics also remains inadequate as a tool for coping with a number of serious questions which also arise in the interpretation of a sacred or authoritative text, or even of a text for which historical inquiries are constructive. We need the resources and models *both* of the post-Julicher era *and* of the post-Jeremias era.

In particular, the model of speech as action serves to clarify a variety of familiar problems in interpretation, even though it does not offer a comprehensive model for all hermeneutical problems. The term "action *model*" is a little broader than "speech-act," since we are not restricting the concept to the particular ways in which it is used in the work of Austin and Searle. On the other hand, "action theory" embraces a broader approach to hermeneutical questions than I have in view here and raises philosophical issues about causality and agency which, once again, are not in view here. Wittgenstein observed that using language was as much a part of the natural history of humankind as walking, eating, or playing. This is our point. The actions surrounding, and in a sense performed by, a text are multiple. The author or speaker is responsible for this action, and it is patently false to claim that human action can have nothing to do with purpose, intention, situation, or goal.

On the other hand, once the text comes to occupy a place in tradition and to be read in times or places different from those in which it was spoken or written, further dimensions of action and their effects begin to emerge. Readers may "use" the text for purposes not envisaged by the author, and because such "uses" also remain personal actions their propriety may be judged by certain criteria of responsibility. The action model allows us to separate out different levels and dimensions of language use without necessarily opening the door to the mistaken view that the "meaning" of a text is simply what any reader cares to do with it. Some actions seem more appropriate than others. If language is a tool, what was that tool designed to do? Is it now being used responsibly? It is *possible* to make a text "mean" what the reader uses it to mean, just as it it *possible* to use a chisel as a screwdriver. In such a case of forced misapplication it is not enough to answer "But the chisel turned the screw effectively"—though such an answer may shed light on certain interpretive practices and their basis. We must begin further back, inquiring how this action model has a bearing on our discussion up to this point.

One fundamental principle of speech-act theory is that a text may perform *multiple* functions. A narrative, for example, seldom merely narrates. It may also inform, direct, nourish a sense of community solidarity on the basis of corporate memory, produce grief or joy, or constitute an act of celebration. The parables do in the first place project a narrative world as the necessary condition for the effective operation of other actions, including linguistic acts. From a philosophical viewpoint, Heidegger most strikingly gave expression to the insight in his later work that an artistic creation performs the act of gathering together into a single unit the elements of a world *into* which a person may imaginatively enter and *by* and *through* which understanding can occur at a deeper level than a merely conceptual consciousness.[81] Thus a Greek temple, for example, "opens up a world."[82] *Saying* "gathers all things up" and invites participation and entry into a projected or founded world which has been constructed through a "gathering call."[83] In literature Heidegger expounds this principle with reference to a range of poetry from Sophocles to Stefan George, and from Georg Trakl to Friedrich Hölderlin. He does not employ the term "speech-act," but it is fundamental to his approach that creative language is seen not as idea but as event.

Ernst Fuchs takes up this approach in his interpretation of the parables. The parables construct a narrative world that becomes a meeting ground between Jesus and the hearer; Jesus enters the hearer's world and stands alongside the hearer *within* the world of the parable. But the eventfulness of language is not exhausted in the act of constructing a narrative world. If the hearer is able to move, with Jesus, from the picture itself to that to which the picture points, then the language-event *(Sprachereignis)* becomes also a *call,* a *demand,* a *pledge,* a *promise,* an *undertaking,* a *warning,* a saving *act.*[84] For example, in the parable of the laborers in the vineyard (Matthew 20:1-6) Jesus constructs a narrative world in which the hearer is already at home. Work is hard, and unemployment is a hazard for casual laborers. The hearers are delighted that employment is found for all the laborers, but naturally they expect that those who have worked longest will receive more than those who began work only at the eleventh hour. Caught up in this world of the hopes of the laborers, the hearer experiences shock and consternation when the predictable laws of this world are shattered. The laborers all receive the same, for grace subverts and relativizes law and justice. This is very different from merely "teaching" grace, however. It is not "the pallid requirement that sinful men should believe in God's kindness."[85] In the more recent terminology of Dan Otto Via, the narrative world both constitutes and generates action (and not merely concepts) because it makes possible a "pre-philosophical living through of experience."[86] The actions of the narrative then take place *on* the reader, and the act of narrating may be accompanied by other dimensions of the speech-act such as warning, persuading, assuring, or transforming.

These distinctions become clearer when we take account of Austin's contrast between perlocutionary and illocutionary speech-acts. A number of biblical and literary scholars have blurred this important distinction by describing all speech-acts as "performative" language. But while a perlocutionary speech-act is performative *by* saying something, an illocutionary utterance performs an act *in* saying something.[87] This distinction is roughly parallel to Nicholas Wolterstorff's contrast between utterances which causally constitute or generate acts and those which effectively count *as* acts. The former operate at the level of psychological persuasion or causal force. Parables which are narrated (first act: setting up a narrative world) may also act as warnings or promises (second act) which in turn rest upon presuppositions about states of affairs. When the reader infers these presuppositions, the parable indirectly or implicitly puts forward a cognitive truth-claim.

We may now apply these distinctions to the problems of reader-response theory and recontextualization. Can a parable "change its meaning"? Does recontextualization into the reader's situation make it "say something different?" It now appears that the answer must be neither "no" alone (parables used only for historical reconstruction) nor simply "yes" (reader-response theory), but *both* yes *and* no, depending on which level or dimension of the speech-act is under consideration, and for what purpose any given "reading" is carried out.

The older models which try to cope with this problem—and we may briefly distinguish four—are inadequate. First, it has become customary in biblical studies to distinguish between "past" and "present" meaning; Dennis Nineham and recently Raymond Brown use this model.[88] But in the end this tidy distinction leaves an unbridgeable gap between exegesis and theology. Brown quite rightly insists that we should not decide exegetical questions on the basis of dogma, but beneath his argument lies an implicit fact-value distinction. What the text of the Bible "meant" emerges through descriptive historical and philological science; what it "means" is its theological value for the life of the church. His model tells us nothing helpful about the relation between the two, unless we already believe that whatever emerges in theological tradition is a natural and congruent recontextualization of the text. In effect, it is a biblical scholar's version of the second model, which we find in E. D. Hirsch, of a clear-cut contrast between meaning and application. But a number of writers, including most convincingly David Couzens Hoy, have shown that this contrast depends on a circular argument about the *accessibility* of "meaning" as over against interpretation.[89] A third model, put forward by Gadamer, is that of an "effective history" in which the distinction between meaning and application disappears. But in spite of the enormous value of Gadamer's work, he can leave no room for hermeneutical norms of a kind which would help us to decide what might constitute *responsible* interpretation in any given case. On his own admission, his hermeneutics yields no more than a description of the interpretive process. Finally, the reader-oriented models of Rorty and Fish, while rightly rejecting a falsely optimistic textual objectivism, leave us in an entirely relativistic world where we can do no more than live out our interpretive activities without even asking questions about validity, norms, or truth in any ultimately serious sense.

By contrast, the action model helps us to see in what sense recontextualization changes the meaning and in what sense it does not. For example, a statement that asserts a state of affairs retains its assertive function as a statement about the situation which was the case at the time of the utterance. "Caesar crossed the Rubicon" and "Jesus was crucified under Pontius Pilate" do not change in meaning as acts of asserting a state of affairs whether or not they are subsequently recontextualized. Even the three parables of Luke 15, the lost sheep (vv. 1-7), the lost coin (vv. 8-10), and the lost son and the elder brother (vv. 11-32), serve in their Lukan context in effect to assert that God rejoices to welcome the sinner, and at the level of assertion this truth transcends subsequent recontextualization. Nevertheless within the pages of the New Testament the action of the parable of the lost sheep, already a defense against pharisaic criticism of grace (Luke 15:1-7), becomes recontextualized in Matthew as the verbal action of a pastoral charge to care for the weak and erring and "not to despise one of these little ones" (Matthew 18:10-14). The performative act of pastoral charge is derivative from, and congruent with, the actions of the Lukan context, but the recontextualization in Matthew provides a new and different action at a different level of function. Questions about hermeneutical "control" or criteria of congruency are more specific and tangible when applied to the functions of different sorts of acts than the vague and often circular questions about whether some "interpretation" is congruent with the text. (If we could know the answer to this, we should less readily need to raise the question in the first place.) The action model asks not whether *text* and *interpretation* are congruent, but whether the primary action and the truth-claims in which it is embedded have been reduced or changed in different contexts.

At this point it is instructive to examine the purpose of parables, and of models of their meanings, which occur within the New Testament itself. The interpretation of Mark 4:11-12 and its subsequent parables has long been an intractable problem in New Testament studies. We will cite the verses in full: "And when he was alone, those who were about him with the twelve asked him concerning the parables. And he said to them, 'To you has been given the secret of the kingdom of God, but for those outside [Greek *tois exō*] everything is in parables; so that *[hina]* they may indeed see but not perceive *[blepōsin kai mē idōsin],* and may indeed hear but not understand *[akouōsin kai mē syniōsin]; lest [mepōte]* they should turn again, and be forgiven.' " It is noteworthy that this is followed by Jesus' assumption that even the disciples (or Manson/Baird's "crowd of disciples") did not understand the parable of the sower. Jesus proceeds to offer an "interpretation" of this parable.

By way of summary we may distinguish five main views of this difficult passage. First, Jülicher dismissed the idea that Jesus could or would have told a parable "so that they might not perceive." He believed, therefore, that Mark had added that explanation for theological purposes, since only "insiders" could understand and respond to the gospel. This fits in well with Wrede's theory about Mark's theological concerns but is otherwise unsupported by the text. A second approach is to interpret Mark's *hina* in the light of Matthew's *hoti:* Jesus used parables "because" the crowd could not perceive, not "in order that" they might not perceive. However, this view brings its own problems, not least that it is easier to explain Matthew's softening explanation of Mark, rather than Mark's introduction of such a difficult phrase. It is possible that we may ascribe both *hina* and *hoti* to the same Semitic word or idea, but unless *hina* is to be softened to the extent advocated by C. F. D. Moule, this does not solve the problem of Mark's choice of vocabulary. A third explanation is a fully predestinarian understanding of the verse, but if this is so, it seems to be at variance with the general thrust of what is said about Jesus' preaching in the synoptic Gospels. A fourth way forward suggested by a number of interpreters is to discard the specific allusion to parables in favor of understanding the passage to refer more broadly to Jesus' teaching. But this also raises difficulties and is unnecessary.

A fifth, and more satisfactory explanation, is to see elements of both judgment and blessing in these words. Jesus used parables *in order to prevent premature understanding unaccompanied by inner change.* This includes the notion of judgment (implied here by the allusion to Israel's blindness in the Old Testament), since a person who has neither the will nor the capacity to understand suffers the inbuilt penalty which this failure carries with it. But it also embraces compassion and mercy, for the parables also prevent a premature and superficial rejection of the gospel. The crowd of opponents can indeed "see" *that* they are challenged; but only when they are grasped by the parable at a more than merely superficial conscious level is response precipitated in such a way that they "see" its full *point.* The parable functions in such a way as to prevent a superficial rejection of Jesus' person and message merely on the basis of a shallow assent to current Jewish ideas, and it achieves this by its action. A parable may even allow progressive levels of understanding as the pieces gradually fall into place and the hearer's perceptions are duly revised and transformed.

These *progressive levels of understanding* in practice take shape as the experiencing of *progressive levels of linguistic or textual action.* Who can say in advance of the experience whether the parable of the lost sheep in its Matthean context will first be read as an exhortation to pastoral responsibility, or, on the basis of a prior knowledge of Luke, whether it will first be read as an assertion of God's grace toward sinners which should then be reflected in the attitudes of Christian leaders? The Bible may be understood on different levels. In other words, its text performs a variety of actions on the reader, and the reader's repertoire of interpretive responses themselves constitute a varied range of actions. But not all interpretive acts of reading are equally responsible. The interpretation already conveyed alongside the parable in the Gospel of Thomas cannot be said to be responsible since it forces the text to perform additional acts of theological assertion which have no direct or even indirect connection with the actions performed by the language of Jesus and the truth-claims which make Jesus' own speech-act precisely his *act.* Questions about the nature of the person and ministry of Jesus, including the situations of his utterances and audiences, do provide controls over the range of acts which the text may perform when it is interpreted responsibly.

Indeed, interpretive *responsibility* emerges here as a major and constructive hermeneutical category. It is sometimes fruitless to ask whether a text can be taken to mean something without asking whether we can take it to mean this *responsibly*. But responsibility also depends on purpose and situation. A piano *can* be used for firewood, and in most circumstances such actions would be irresponsible. But if one were dying of cold, stranded on an ice floe in the Arctic Ocean, it might conceivably become a responsible act to set fire even to a Steinway. In certain situations, either in the context of religious devotion or of some other hypothetical situation, the use of a text may seem to be vindicated solely by its effect in terms of reader-response. But such a vindication is not appropriate when some claim is being made for the authoritative role of the text in shaping thought and conduct. Unusual and anomalous situations are parasitic upon the customary use of more broadly based criteria in more regular situations. We earlier discussed, for example, Irenaeus's use of the parable of the laborers in the vineyard. Was this use "responsible"? Did the gnostic challenge provide a special situation which made his concern for the hermeneutical principle of the rule of faith the overridingly "responsible" concern? Whatever our answer about Irenaeus's situation, we can say that for *us* in the twentieth century this could no longer remain a responsible interpretation. For the act of describing God's progressive calls in the history of the world is not at any level an act of this parable.

The model of action helps us forward, then, with constructive questions and criteria enabling us to break the spell of some of the well-worn models which has dominated hermeneutical theory and sometimes brought confusion and a sense of stalemate. Most significantly, this model allows us to see that a variety of actions may occur in a text at the same time and that recontextualization affects the relative priority of these operations in relation to one another. This does not mean, however, that the Bible becomes the nose of wax about which Luther warned, as if it could be pushed into any shape that the reader may fancy. Nor does it mean that action or speech-acts provide a comprehensive model for the solution of all hermeneutical problems. No theoretical model provided by hermeneutical theory can obviate the need first and foremost to look at the text itself in its linguistic and historical particularity.

NOTES

Introduction

1. "Criticism as Pure Speculation," in *The Intent of the Critic,* ed. Donald A. Stauffer (Princeton: Princeton University Press, 1941); rpt. in *Criticism: The Major Statements,* ed. Charles Kaplan (New York: St. Martin's Press, 1975), p. 503.

Notes to Part I

1. The term "hermeneutics" has come to mean many different things. Three of the most impressive attempts to define and explain the word are Richard Palmer, *Hermeneutics: Interpretation Theory in Schleiermacher, Dilthey, Heidegger, and Gadamer* (Evanston: Northwestern University Press, 1969); Anthony C. Thiselton, *The Two Horizons: New Testament Hermeneutics and Philosophical Description* (Grand Rapids: Eerdmans, 1980); and Paul Ricoeur, *Hermeneutics and the Human Sciences: Essays on Language, Action and Interpretation,* trans. and ed. John B. Thompson (Cambridge: Cambridge University Press, 1981). See also Richard J. Bernstein, *Beyond Objectivism and Relativism: Science, Hermeneutics, and Praxis* (Philadelphia: University of Pennsylvania Press, 1983).

2. St. Augustine, *Confessions,* trans. Rex Warner (New York: New American Library, 1963), pp. 182-83.

3. René Descartes, *Meditations on First Philosophy,* in *Philosophical Writings,* trans. and ed. Norman Kemp Smith (London: Macmillan, 1952), pp. 196-97.

4. Helmut Thielicke, *The Evangelical Faith,* vol. 1, trans. and ed. Geoffrey Bromiley (Grand Rapids: Eerdmans, 1974), pp. 34, 35; for further discussions of Cartesianism (and the foundationalism it fostered) see: Paul Ricoeur, *The Symbolism of Evil,* trans. Emerson Buchanan (Boston: Beacon Press, 1967); Hans-Georg Gadamer, *Truth and Method,* translation edited by Garrett Barden and John Cumming (New York: Continuum, 1975);

Richard Rorty, *Philosophy and the Mirror of Nature* (Princeton: Princeton University Press, 1979); and Nicholas Wolterstorff, *Reason within the Bounds of Religion,* 2nd ed. (Grand Rapids: Eerdmans, 1984). For an exploration of the relationship of Cartesian themes to contemporary literary theory, see Gerald L. Bruns, *Inventions: Writing, Textuality and Understanding in Literary History* (New Haven: Yale University Press, 1982).

5. See Francis Bacon, *Novum Organum,* ed. Thomas Fowler (Oxford: Clarendon Press, 1889), and *The Advancement of Science,* ed. William Aldis Wright (Oxford: Clarendon Press, 1900).

6. Franklin L. Baumer, *Modern European Thought* (New York: Macmillan, 1977), p. 32.

7. Ibid., p. 130.

8. Gadamer, *Truth and Method,* pp. 239-40.

9. Ibid., p. 240.

10. Jerome Stolnitz, "On the Origins of 'Aesthetic Disinterestedness,' " *Journal of Aesthetics and Art Criticism,* 20 (1961), 132. For an introduction to Shaftesbury which places him in a broad context, see Basil Willey, *The Eighteenth-Century Background* (Boston: Beacon Press, 1961), pp. 57-75.

11. For the background of modern aesthetic theory, see, among many other studies, M. H. Abrams, *The Mirror and the Lamp: Romantic Theory and the Critical Tradition* (London: Oxford University Press, 1953); Ernest Tuveson, *The Imagination as a Means of Grace: Locke and the Aesthetics of Romanticism* (Berkeley: University of California Press, 1960); Gadamer, *Truth and Method,* pp. 39-90; Paul Oscar Kristeller, "The Modern System of the Arts: A Study in the History of Aesthetics," *Journal of the History of Ideas,* 12 (1951), 496-527, 13 (1952), 13-46; Nicholas Wolterstorff, *Art in Action* (Grand Rapids: Eerdmans, 1980); and Terry Eagleton, *Literary Theory: An Introduction* (Minneapolis: University of Minnesota Press, 1983), pp. 1-53. The developments discussed in these works represent an astonishing shift in the history of the arts. M. H. Abrams writes: "To many of us, such assertions also seem to be patent truths, confirmed by our ordinary experience of works of art. The historical facts, however, should give us pause. For some two thousand years of theoretical concern with these matters, it occurred to no thinker to claim that a human artifact is to be contemplated disinterestedly, for its own sake, as its own end and for its internal values, without reference to things, human beings, purposes, or effects outside its sufficient and autonomous self." "Kant and the Theology of Art," *Notre Dame English Journal,* 13 (1981), 76.

12. Immanuel Kant, *Critique of Judgment,* trans. James C. Meredith, in *The Philosophy of Kant,* ed. Carl J. Friedrich (New York: Modern Library, 1949), p. 290. For a succinct discussion of Kantian aesthetics, see Roger Scruton, *Kant* (Oxford: Oxford University Press, 1982), pp. 78-91.

13. Ibid., p. 292.

14. Ibid., p. 293. "Nietzsche long ago remarked that 'Kant, like all philosophers, instead of viewing the issue from the side of the artist, envisaged art and beauty solely from the "spectator's" point of view.' Nietzsche is right, in that Kant takes as paradigmatic an encounter between a perceiver and an object which is held isolatedly in attention, and is 'immediately'—that is without intervening thought, or reference to a 'concept'—experienced pleasurably as being 'beautiful,' or as possessing 'aesthetic quality' *[aesthetische Beschaffenheit].* But I would specify that Kant's model for analyzing this encounter is not the Addisonian spectator, but a contemplator—a model with a very different philosophical provenience. In Kant's summary statement: a 'pure' judgment of taste combines delight or aversion immediately with the bare contemplation *[blossen Betrachtung]* of the object irrespective of its use or of any end. Such a judgment, it should be remarked, is 'pure' in that it satisfies all, and only, the necessary and sufficient criteria for being accounted an aesthetic judgment—without, that is, any superfluous or conflicting elements" (Abrams, "Kant and the Theology of Art," p. 81).

15. Kant, *Critique of Judgment*, p. 284. Frank Lentricchia observes that Kant's "intention of isolating the distinctive character of the aesthetic experience was admirable, but his analysis resulted in mere isolation. By barring that experience from the truth of the phenomenal world, while allowing art's fictional world entertainment value, he became the philosophical father of an enervating aestheticism which ultimately subverts what it would celebrate" *(After the New Criticism* [Chicago: University of Chicago Press, 1980], p. 41).

16. M. H. Abrams, *Natural Supernaturalism: Tradition and Revolution in Romantic Literature* (New York: W.W. Norton, 1971; Norton Library, 1973), p. 13.

17. Cited by Abrams in "Wordsworth's Prospectus for The Recluse," in *Natural Supernaturalism,* p. 467.

18. Abrams, *Natural Supernaturalism,* p. 332. See also Harold Bloom, *The Visionary Company: A Reading of English Romantic Poetry,* rev. ed. (Ithaca: Cornell University Press, 1971); Clarke Garrett, *Respectable Folly: Millenarians and the French Revolution* (Baltimore: Johns Hopkins University Press, 1975); Henry F. May, *The Enlightenment in America* (Oxford: Oxford University Press, 1976), pp. 153-96; and Nathan O. Hatch, *The Sacred Cause of Liberty: Republican Thought and the Millennium in Revolutionary New England* (New Haven: Yale University Press, 1977), pp. 21-54.

19. "Faith in an apocalypse by revelation had been replaced by faith in an apocalypse by revolution, and this now gave way to faith in an apocalypse by imagination or cognition. In the ruling two-term frame of Romantic thought, the mind of man confronts the old heaven and earth and possesses within itself the power, if it will but recognize and avail itself of the power, to transform them into a new heaven and new earth, by means of a total revolution of consciousness" (Abrams, *Natural Supernaturalism,* p. 334). Two recent studies which make a similar argument in great detail are Eagleton, *Literary Theory: An Introduction,* and Jerome McGann, *The Romantic Ideology: A Critical Investigation* (Chicago: University of Chicago Press, 1983).

20. Samuel Taylor Coleridge, *Biographia Literaria,* in *The Portable Coleridge,* ed. I. A. Richards (New York: Viking, 1950), p. 522.

21. Ibid., p. 516; *The Letters of John Keats,* vol. 1, ed. Hyder E. Rollins (Cambridge: Harvard University Press, 1958), p. 193; *The Poems of Emily Dickinson,* ed. Thomas Johnson (Cambridge: Belknap Press, 1963), p. 335; *The Selected Writings of Walter Pater,* ed. Harold Bloom (New York: New American Library, 1974), pp. 105-6; *Selected Prose of Robert Frost,* ed. Hyde Cox and Edward Connery Lathem (New York: Holt, Rinehart and Winston, 1959), p. 18.

22. Walter Ong, "From Rhetorical Culture to New Criticism: The Poem as a Closed Field," in *The Possibilities of Order: Cleanth Brooks and His Work,* ed. Lewis P. Simpson (Baton Rouge: Louisiana State University Press, 1976), p. 160. For examples of the way in which the doctrine of the poem as a closed field has influenced American New Criticism, see John Crowe Ransom, *Beating the Bushes: Selected Essays 1941-1970* (New York: New Directions, 1972), and René Wellek and Austin Warren, *Theory of Literature,* 3rd ed. rev. (New York: Harcourt Brace Jovanovich, 1977), pp. 20-37.

23. Ibid., p. 161.

24. Ibid., pp. 160-61.

25. Northrop Frye, *Anatomy of Criticism: Four Essays* (Princeton: Princeton University Press, 1957; paperback edition, 1971), pp. 3-29.

26. Ibid., p. 74.

27. Ibid., p. 75.

28. Northrop Frye, *The Educated Imagination* (Bloomington: Indiana University Press, 1964), pp. 32-33.

29. Ibid., p. 80.

30. Gilbert Chinard, "The American Dream," in *Literary History of the United States,* 4th ed. rev., ed. Robert E. Spiller et al. (New York: Macmillan, 1974), p. 192.

On the subject of America as Eden or the New Jerusalem, see Henry Nash Smith, *Virgin Land: The American West as Symbol and Myth* (Cambridge: Harvard University Press, 1950); R. W. B. Lewis, *The American Adam: Innocence, Tragedy, and Tradition in the Nineteenth Century* (Chicago: University of Chicago Press, 1955); and Perry Miller, *Errand into the Wilderness* (Cambridge: Belknap Press, 1956).

31. John Winthrop, "A Model of Christian Charity," in *The Norton Anthology of American Literature,* vol. 1, 2nd ed., ed. Nina Baym et al. (New York: W.W. Norton, 1985), p. 24.

32. Ibid., p. 45.

33. J. Hector St. John de Crèvecoeur, *Letters from an American Farmer,* "Letter III: What Is an American?" in *Letters from an American Farmer and Sketches of 18th-Century America,* ed. Albert E. Stone (New York: Penguin, 1981), pp. 73-74.

34. Ibid., p. 70.

35. Karl Barth, *Protestant Thought: From Rousseau to Ritschl,* trans. Brian Cozens (New York: Simon and Schuster, 1969), p. 11.

36. Ibid., p. 17.

37. Ralph Waldo Emerson, "Self-Reliance," in *Ralph Waldo Emerson: Essays and Lectures* (New York: The Library of America, 1983), p. 270.

38. Emerson, "The American Scholar," in ibid., p. 57.

39. Emerson, "Self-Reliance," in ibid., p. 259.

40. Emerson, "The Divinity School Address," in ibid., pp. 88, 81.

41. Ibid., pp. 88-89.

42. Ibid., p. 83.

43. Emerson, "The American Scholar," in ibid., p. 70.

44. Emerson, "Self-Reliance," in ibid., p. 259.

45. Nathaniel Hawthorne, *The Scarlet Letter,* in *Nathaniel Hawthorne: Novels* (New York: The Library of America, 1983), p. 261. For my reading of *The Scarlet Letter* I am especially indebted to William C. Spengemann, *The Adventurous Muse: The Poetics of American Fiction, 1789-1900* (New Haven: Yale University Press, 1977), pp. 160-72.

46. Emerson, "Experience," in *Emerson: Essays and Lectures,* p. 473.

47. Of the numerous studies on this subject, see especially D. H. Meyer, *The Instructed Conscience: The Shaping of the American National Ethic* (Philadelphia: University of Pennsylvania Press, 1972); May, *The Enlightenment in America;* Theodore Dwight Bozeman, *Protestants in an Age of Science: The Baconian Ideal and Antebellum American Religious Thought* (Chapel Hill: University of North Carolina Press, 1977); and George M. Marsden, "Everyone One's Own Interpreter?: The Bible, Science, and Authority in Mid-Nineteenth-Century America," in *The Bible in America,* ed. Nathan O. Hatch and Mark A. Noll (New York: Oxford University Press, 1982), pp. 79-100. For the implications of recent developments in this area, see Mark A. Noll, "Evangelicals and the Study of the Bible," in *Evangelicalism and Modern America,* ed. George Marsden (Grand Rapids: Eerdmans, 1984), pp. 103-21.

48. *America,* ed. Perry Miller (Cambridge: Belknap Press, 1961), pp. 31-32.

49. In *Protestants in an Age of Science,* Bozeman documents the enshrinement of "Lord Bacon" and the irresistible force of "the Baconian juggernaut" in nineteenth-century America. See especially pp. 3-31 and 132-59.

50. As quoted in Bozeman, p. 155.

51. Sydney Ahlstrom, *A Religious History of the American People,* vol. 1 (Garden City, N.Y.: Image Books, 1975), p. 543.

52. As quoted in Nathan O. Hatch, *"Sola Scriptura* and *Novus Ordo Seclorum,"* in *The Bible in America,* pp. 73-74.

53. As quoted in ibid., pp. 73-74.

54. Roger Scruton, *From Descartes to Wittgenstein: A Short History of Modern*

Philosophy (New York: Harper and Row, 1982), p. 284. In *Philosophy and the Mirror of Nature,* Richard Rorty ties the rise of interest in hermeneutics to the collapse of Cartesian foundationalism. Rorty speaks of corpses, parasites, coping, and conversation. "Hermeneutics . . . is what we get when we are no longer epistemological," he claims. Or, to use his metaphors, hermeneutics is the parasite that lives in and off the dead body of epistemology; it is the means we have of coping, through lively talk and poetic flights of fancy, with the fact that our minds have nothing in which to believe and our words have nothing to which they can or do correspond. The hermeneut, then, is the parasite who lives in the rotting body of Western tradition and carries on comforting conversations in the pale light given off by the embers of belief.

Many who encounter hermeneutical theory fear the very thing that Rorty seems to welcome with unabashed glee; they fear that the collapse of foundationalism and Cartesian certainty lead to the impossibility of acquiring trustworthy knowledge and to the absurdity of questions about truth. But one can argue that Christian theism and human knowledge do not collapse if Cartesianism and foundationalism do. Three very different yet complementary works make this claim. They are Helmut Thielicke, *Evangelical Theology,* vol. 1; Nicholas Wolterstorff, *Reason within the Bounds of Religion;* and Paul Ricoeur, "Toward a Hermeneutic of the Idea of Revelation," trans. David Pellauer, *Harvard Theological Review,* 70 (1970), 1-37.

55. Gadamer, *Truth and Method,* p. 244.

56. Ibid., pp. 239-40.

57. Ibid., p. 245.

58. Paul Ricoeur, "The Task of Hermeneutics," trans. David Pellauer, in *Heidegger and Modern Philosophy,* ed. Michael Murray (New Haven: Yale University Press, 1978), p. 152. The work of Gadamer and Ricoeur displays a clear indebtedness to Heidegger, whose major work on the subject of hermeneutics is the difficult *Being and Time,* trans. John Macquarrie and Edward Robinson (New York: Harper and Row, 1962). For a lucid introduction to Heidegger, see George Steiner, *Martin Heidegger* (New York: Penguin, 1980).

59. Ricoeur, *The Symbolism of Evil,* p. 348. Two recent books by Ricoeur in effect bring together the various strands of the argument he has developed over the last three decades: *The Rule of Metaphor,* trans. Robert Czerny with Kathleen McLaughlin and John Costello, S.J. (Toronto: University of Toronto Press, 1977), and *Time and Narrative,* vol. 1, trans. Kathleen McLaughlin and David Pellauer (Chicago: University of Chicago Press, 1984).

60. Gadamer, *Truth and Method,* p. 338.

61. Ludwig Wittgenstein, *Philosophical Investigations,* trans. G. E. M. Anscombe (Oxford: Basil Blackwell, 1953), p. 6.

62. Ibid., p. 11.

63. Ibid., p. 8.

64. Ibid., p. 81.

65. Thiselton, *The Two Horizons,* p. 381.

66. Ibid., p. 382.

67. Ricoeur, *Symbolism of Evil,* p. 352.

68. Ibid., p. 356.

69. Hans-Georg Gadamer, *Philosophical Hermeneutics,* trans. and ed. David E. Linge (Berkeley: University of California Press, 1976), p. 64.

70. Emerson, "The American Scholar," in *Emerson: Essays and Lectures,* p. 59.

71. Stanley Fish, *Is There a Text in This Class? The Authority of Interpretive Communities* (Cambridge: Harvard University Press, 1980).

72. Paul Althaus, *The Theology of Martin Luther,* trans. Robert Schultz (Philadelphia: Fortress, 1966), p. 335.

73. Paul Ricoeur, *Interpretation Theory: Discourse and the Surplus of Meaning* (Fort

Worth: Texas Christian University Press, 1976), p. 79. See also Bernstein, *Beyond Objectivism and Relativism* (cf. n. 1).

Notes to Part II

1. Edward Said uses the term *textuality* to identify the concerns of modern theorists who hold that hermeneutical issues are defined by the text itself as opposed to the text's relation to the world (cf. *The World, the Text, and the Critic* [Cambridge: Harvard University Press, 1983], pp. 3-4, 130, 173, 215 et passim). The position that we will develop is much more compatible with Said's than with the positions he criticizes, but a theory of textuality is needed if hermeneutics is not to be relativized by too exclusive a stress on reader-response and political praxis. Like Said, we reject theories which build on the notion of textual autonomy, and we propose a theory in which textuality is inconceivable apart from the multifarious relationships of texts to the world surrounding the text. Our theory aims to bridge the gap between what Paul de Man identifies as the respective concerns of of hermeneutics and poetics (cf. "Introduction" to Hans Robert Jauss, *Toward an Aesthetics of Reception,* trans. Timothy Bahti [Minneapolis: University of Minnesota Press, 1982], p. ix). According to de Man's nomenclature (which is derived from the Konstanz series published under the general title *Poetik und Hermeneutik),* hermeneutics is concerned with interpreting particular texts whereas poetics is concerned with the nature of linguistic entities. De Man observes that American critics typically are drawn to the hermeneutical tasks (How should we interpret this text?) and become impatient with poetics (What is a text?). Hermeneutics, however, is often used in a broader sense—sometimes called philosophical hermeneutics—which embraces both theoretical and practical concerns. Our theory of textuality is part of a hermeneutical theory in this broad sense and is offered as an attempt to show the relation between the theoretical issues of philosophical hermeneutics and the practical goals of interpretation. A textual theory which is philosophically viable should help to clarify the link between general poetics and practical methodology as well as the tie which binds texts to the world.

2. Paul de Man, *Allegories of Reading: Figural Language in Rousseau, Nietzsche, Rilke, and Proust* (New Haven: Yale University Press, 1979), p. 37.

3. Matthew Arnold, "The Study of Poetry," in *Essays in Criticism: Second Series* (1880), rpt. in *Criticism: The Major Statements,* ed. Charles Kaplan (New York: St. Martin's Press, 1975), p. 404; Hippolyte-Adolphe Taine, "Introduction," *History of English Literature* (1863), rpt. in *Criticism: The Major Texts,* ed. Walter Jackson Bate (New York: Harcourt Brace Jovanovich, 1970), p. 506; Henry James, "The Art of Fiction" (1884), rpt. in *Criticism: The Major Statements,* ed. Kaplan, p. 437; Robert Frost, "The Figure a Poem Makes" (1939), rpt. in *Robert Frost: Poetry and Prose,* ed. Edward C. Lathem and Lawrence Thompson (New York: Holt, Rinehart, and Winston, Inc., 1972), p. 394; William Carlos Williams, "A Sort of Song," in *The William Carlos Williams Reader,* ed. M. L. Rosenthal (New York: New Directions, 1966), pp. 46-47; Wallace Stevens, *Opus Posthumous* (New York: Alfred A. Knopf, 1966), p. 159; T. S. Eliot, "The Modern Mind," in *The Use of Poetry and the Use of Criticism* (1933; rpt. London: Faber and Faber, 1955), p. 139.

4. René Wellek and Austin Warren, *Theory of Literature,* 3rd ed. (New York: Harcourt Brace Jovanovich, 1977), p. 22.

5. Northrop Frye, *Anatomy of Criticism: Four Essays* (Princeton: Princeton University Press, 1957), p. 352.

6. David Bleich, *Subjective Criticism* (Baltimore: The Johns Hopkins University Press, 1978), p. 37.

7. John M. Ellis, *The Theory of Literary Criticism: A Logical Analysis* (Berkeley: University of California Press, 1974), p. 42.

8. De Man, *Allegories of Reading,* p. 10.

9. For hermeneutics, the most pertinent developments in action theory are to be found in speech-action theorists in the tradition of J. R. Austin and John Searle and in philosophers like Alvin Goldman, *A Theory of Human Action* (Englewood Cliffs, N.J.: Prentice-Hall, 1970), and Nicholas Wolterstorff, *Works and Worlds of Art* (Oxford: Clarendon Press, 1980).

10. His influence is evident in biblical studies as well as in literary criticism. Cf. *Derrida and Biblical Studies (Semeia 23,* 1982), ed. Robert Detweiler.

11. Jacques Derrida, "White Mythology: Metaphor in the Text of Philosophy," *New Literary History,* 6 (Autumn 1974), p. 74.

12. Jacques Derrida, *Of Grammatology,* trans. Gayatri Chakravorty Spivak (Baltimore: The Johns Hopkins University Press, 1974), pp. 3, 7-10, et passim. The word *writing* will appear in quotation marks to indicate Derrida's special use of it. For its more ordinary use as inscribed language, quotation marks will not be used.

13. Ibid., pp. 18, 46-47, 74-75, et passim.

14. Ibid., p. 24, et passim.

15. Ibid., pp. 23, 66, et passim, and *Writing and Difference,* trans. Alan Bass (Chicago: University of Chicago Press, 1978), passim.

16. Richard Rorty, *Philosophy and the Mirror of Nature* (Princeton: Princeton University Press, 1979).

17. De Man, *Allegories of Reading,* p. 10.

18. Ibid., p. 13.

19. Ibid., p. 17.

20. Ibid.

21. Ibid., p. 19.

22. Ibid., p. 45.

23. Ibid., pp. 111, 152-53, and 161.

24. Ibid., p. 208.

25. Ibid., p. 194.

26. Ibid., p. 50.

27. Ferdinand de Saussure, *Course in General Linguistics,* trans. Wade Baskin, ed. Charles Bally, Albert Sechehaye, and Albert Riedlinger (New York: The Philosophical Library, 1959; rpt. McGraw-Hill, paperback edition, 1966).

28. Cf. Fredric Jameson, *The Political Unconscious: Narrative as a Socially Symbolic Act* (Ithaca: Cornell University Press, 1981); T. K. Seung, *Structuralism and Hermeneutics* (New York: Columbia University Press, 1982); Charles Altieri, *Act and Quality: A Theory of Literary Meaning and Humanistic Understanding* (Amherst: University of Massachusetts Press, 1981); Gerald L. Bruns, *Inventions: Writing, Textuality, and Understanding in Literary History* (New Haven: Yale University Press, 1982); Josue V. Harari, ed., *Textual Strategies: Perspectives in Post-Structuralist Criticism* (Ithaca: Cornell University Press, 1979); Edward W. Said, *Beginnings: Intention and Method* (Baltimore: The Johns Hopkins University Press, 1975).

29. Wolterstorff, *Works and Worlds of Art,* pp. x, 15-16. Cf. Wolterstorff, *Art in Action: Toward a Christian Aesthetic* (Grand Rapids: Eerdmans, 1980), p. 14.

30. Cf. "Are Texts Autonomous? An Interaction with the Hermeneutic of Paul Ricoeur," *Aesthetics: Proceedings of the 8th International Wittgenstein Symposium* (Vienna: Holder Pichler-Tempsky, 1984), pp. 139-52.

31. Cf. Richard E. Palmer, "What Are We *Doing* When We Interpret a Text?" *Eros,* 7 (1980), 1047: "Interpretation *is* an 'action'; it therefore has the structure of an action: purpose, a thing done, a change effected, a context of resistances, conditions, etc."

32. Roman Ingarden, *The Literary Work of Art: An Investigation on the Borderlines of Ontology, Logic, and Theory of Literature,* trans. George C. Grabowicz (Evanston: Northwestern University Press, 1973).

33. Paul Ricoeur, *Hermeneutics and the Human Sciences: Essays on Language, Action, and Interpretation,* trans. and ed. John B. Thompson (Cambridge: Cambridge University Press, 1981), esp. pp. 131-44, 197, 221. Cf. Ricoeur, *Interpretation Theory* (Fort Worth: Texas Christian University Press, 1976).

34. Ingarden, *The Literary Work of Art,* p. 230.

35. Ibid., p. 130.

36. Walker Gibson, "Authors, Speakers, Readers, and Mock Readers," *College English,* 11 (1950), 265-69.

37. A theory of conceptual reference seems to stand behind the position advocated by David Bleich in his *Subjective Criticism.* Although he does not speak of the problem of reference directly, his conception of language-meaning implies that what language talks *about* is established by and in consciousness: "The stability of consciousness depends on the stability of our language" (p. 37). "The subjective paradigm says that the level of primary reality is symbolic because that is how the organ of consciousness functions. Consciousness takes real objects for granted and directs its efforts either toward symbolic manipulation of real objects or toward symbolic manipulation of objects of its own creation—symbolic objects. In either case reality is *defined* symbolically" (p. 88). "Neither a reader nor an observer of a reader can confuse the reader's conception of this experience forming thoughts from the reading of words with any real object. There is no need, therefore, to define a special space in which to locate the 'union of reader and text.' The symbolization of the text and the interpretive resymbolization, if any, are both located in the reader's mind" (p. 113).

38. Tzvetan Todorov, *The Poetics of Prose,* trans. Richard Howard (Ithaca: Cornell University Press, 1977), pp. 20-21.

39. John Ellis, *The Theory of Literary Criticism,* pp. 26, 12.

40. Michael Riffaterre, *Semiotics of Poetry* (Bloomington: Indiana University Press, 1978), pp. 7, 13.

41. Wolfgang Iser, *The Act of Reading: A Theory of Aesthetic Response* (Baltimore: The Johns Hopkins University Press, 1978).

42. Ibid., p. 24.

43. Ibid., p. 65.

44. Ibid., p. 35.

45. Ibid., p. 68.

46. Ibid., p. 70.

47. Ibid., p. 72.

48. Ibid., p. 109.

49. Ibid., pp. 65-66.

50. Ibid., p. 64.

51. There are exceptions to this. In frequent instances the referents of fictional texts are to be found in the actual world as well as in the fictional world, e.g., London and Paris in Dickens's *A Tale of Two Cities,* Nat Turner in William Styron's *The Confessions of Nat Turner,* etc.

52. The word *alternative* is potentially misleading. Not every fictional work presents us with a worldview that is different from the worldview we hold prior to the reading. Many stories will confirm in us our established ways of seeing the world; indeed, many stories have this as one of their main purposes. I am using *alternative* in a more neutral way to indicate that a new story presents us with a set of characters and situations which we have not encountered in that way before. A new story presents us with an alternative way of seeing the world in the sense that we have not confronted or viewed the world through this means before. Our belief about the world may remain unchanged but the novel gives a new, i.e., alternative, means for seeing it and reflecting on it.

53. It is perhaps worth pointing out that, in a sense not indicated so far, fictional

texts do exist within the actual world and that their fictional worlds are included in the actual world. Rather than conceiving of textual worlds as totally discrete and independent of one another, we should perhaps have in mind a model of "worlds within worlds." In this sense it may also be said that the world of *Don Quixote* is included within the world of John Barth's *The Sot-Weed Factor* when we read that Henry Burlingame III, one of Barth's characters, is reading *Don Quixote*. But this qualification does not change the hermeneutical model that we are proposing, for it is still the fictional world of the novel that is seen in relation to the actual world, however the scope and overlapping of these worlds be understood.

54. W. K. Wimsatt, *Hateful Contraries: Studies in Literature and Criticism* (Lexington: University of Kentucky Press, 1965), p. 217.

55. Wolterstorff, *Art in Action,* pp. 134-35.

56. Ibid., pp. 139-42.

57. Herman Dooyeweerd, *In the Twilight of Western Thought* (Nutley, N.J.: Craig Press, 1960; paperback edition, 1975).

58. At this level a sacred text has a special status. For the Christian church, for example, the Bible is taken as authoritative. The Christian believer does not evaluate the Bible in the sense of subjecting the text to personal criteria of evaluation, but takes what the text says to be the "word of God." The text in a sense evaluates the Christian's views of the world rather than vice versa. The Christian reader takes the biblical paradigms as true.

59. We will not devote a separate section to scientific texts, whether found in the natural or social sciences; but much of what we say about historical texts would be applicable to scientific texts. The primary difference is that a scientific text is not, generally speaking, a narrative text and hence does not, in our sense of the term, project a world. The scientific text purports to describe natural and human phenomena directly and analytically, not primarily by telling a story. Thus, in our view a historical text tells a story and thereby projects a world; its claim is that the events of the projected world coincide with the events of the actual world and that therefore its narrative gives us an account of happenings in the actual world. In contrast a scientific text describes the actual world directly and without the use of a narrative world. Some scientific texts do, of course, employ narrative technique, and, to the extent that they do do, they move along a continuum that stretches from scientific texts to historical texts to fictional texts. Types of texts and genres of texts are best understood on the model of a continuum of related types rather than on a model which makes rigid and discrete categories for scientific, historical, and fictional texts.

60. We are using the terms *kind* or *class* rather than *genre* because the identification of genres and subgenres is very complex and often involves much more than identifying authorial stance. With respect to distinguishing historical and fictional texts as general kinds, the key concept appears to be *authorial stance.*

Notes to Part III

1. Cf. the chapter "The Bible as Literature" in James Barr, *The Bible in the Modern World* (London: SCM, 1973), pp. 53-74.

2. François Bovon and G. Rouiller, eds., *Exegesis: Problems of Method and Exercises in Reading* (Pittsburgh: Pickwick Press, 1978), p. 1.

3. J. L. Austin, *Philosophical Papers,* 2nd ed. (Oxford: Clarendon Press, 1971), pp. 58-60.

4. Ludwig Wittgenstein, *Philosophical Investigations,* trans. G. E. M. Anscombe, 3rd ed. (Oxford: Basil Blackwell, 1967), sect. 132.

5. Martin Heidegger, *Being and Time* (Oxford: Basil Blackwell, 1962), pp. 188-92.

6. Adolf Jülicher, *Die Gleichnisreden Jesu,* 2nd ed. (Freiburg: Mohr, 1899), pp. 1-148.

7. Eta Linnemann, *Parables of Jesus: Introduction and Exposition* (London: SPCK, 1966), p. 5.

8. Rudolf Bultmann, *History of the Synoptic Tradition* (Oxford: Basil Blackwell, 1963), pp. 169-79.

9. John Dominic Crossan, *In Parables: The Challenge of the Historical Jesus* (New York: Harper and Row, 1973), p. 4.

10. Cf. Kendrick Grobel, ed., *The Gospel of Truth* (Nashville: Abingdon, 1960), pp. 129-35; W. C. van Unnik, *Newly Discovered Gnostic Writings* (Naperville, Ill.: Allenson, 1960), p. 35; and S. Laeuchli, *The Language of Faith* (London: Epworth Press, 1962), pp. 67-69.

11. Jülicher, *Die Gleichnisreden Jesu,* vol. 1, pp. 25-118, esp. 52-58 and 92-111.

12. Ibid., pp. 92-111.

13. Ibid.

14. Ibid., p. 495.

15. John Dominic Crossan, *The Dark Interval: Towards a Theology of Story* (Niles, Ill.: Argus, 1975), p. 59.

16. P. S. Hawkins, "Parables as Metaphor," *Christian Scholar's Review,* 12 (1983), 226; cf. 226-36.

17. Hans-Josef Klauck, *Allegorie und Allegorese in synoptischen Gleichnistexten* (Münster: Aschendorff, 1978), pp. 29-31, 132-47, and 354-60. Cf. Hans Weder, *Die Gleichnisse Jesu als Metaphern* (Göttingen: Vandenhoeck und Ruprecht, 1978).

18. Madeleine Boucher, *The Mysterious Parable: A Literary Study* (Washington, D.C.: Catholic Bible Association of America, 1977), pp. 83-84.

19. J. Arthur Baird, *Audience Criticism and the Historical Jesus* (Philadelphia: Westminster Press, 1969).

20. Ibid., p. 47.

21. Ibid., pp. 97-101.

22. Ibid., pp. 103-105.

23. Ibid., p. 134.

24. Cf. J. C. Hurd, Jr., *The Origins of I Corinthians* (London: SPCK, 1965), and Anthony C. Thiselton, "Realized Eschatology at Corinth," *New Testament Studies,* 24 (1978), 510-26.

25. Robert Jewett, *Letters to Pilgrims: A Commentary on the Epistle to the Hebrews* (New York: Pilgrim Press, 1981).

26. Robert M. Fowler, *Loaves and Fishes: The Function of the Feeding Stories in the Gospel of Mark,* Society of Biblical Literature Dissertation Series 54 (Chico, Calif.: Scholars Press, 1981), and R. Alan Culpepper, *Anatomy of the Fourth Gospel: A Study in Literary Design* (Philadelphia: Fortress Press, 1983). Since this manuscript was completed, James L. Resseguie has published a survey of reader-response approaches and their relevance to material in the Gospels ("Reader-Response Criticism and the Synoptic Gospels," *Journal of the American Academy of Religion,* 52 [1984], 307-24). Resseguie's emphasis is largely on a range of approaches in literary theory; he is less explicitly concerned with the standard literature of New Testament scholarship, nor does he concentrate especially on the parables. But he usefully explores the differing textual and reading strategies discussed by such writers as Norman Holland and David Bleich, observing particularly the textual strategies of defamiliarization and entrapment, the role of expectation, and the building of self-identity in the active experience of the reader.

27. Fowler, *Loaves and Fishes,* esp. pp. 91-148; cf. 149-79.

28. Culpepper, *Anatomy of the Fourth Gospel,* p. 233.

29. Cf. esp. Stanley Fish, *Is There a Text in This Class? The Authority of Interpretive Communities* (Cambridge: Harvard University Press, 1980).

30. Roland Barthes, "From Work to Text," and Michel Foucault, "What Is an

Author?" in J. V. Harari, ed., *Textual Strategies: Perspectives in Post-Structuralist Criticism* (Ithaca: Cornell University Press, 1979), pp. 73-81 and 141-60.

31. Cf. Tzvetan Todorov, "Reading as Construction," and P. Maranda, "The Dialectic of Metaphor," in Susan R. Suileman and Inge Crosman, eds., *The Reader in the Text: Essays on Audience and Interpretation* (Princeton: Princeton University Press, 1980), pp. 67-82 and 183-204.

32. Fish, *Is There a Text in This Class?* p. 3.

33. Ibid., p. 12.

34. Ibid., p. 13.

35. Ibid., p. 371.

36. Susan Suileman in Suileman and Crosman, eds., *The Reader in the Text,* p. 3.

37. James M. Robinson, "Hermeneutic Since Barth," in James M. Robinson and J. D. Cobb, eds., *New Frontiers in Theology, II: The New Hermeneutic* (New York: Harper and Row, 1964), pp. 1-77.

38. Ernst Fuchs, *Hermeneutik,* 4th ed. (Tübingen: Mohr, 1970); Gerhard Ebeling, *Word and Faith* (London: SPCK, 1963), and *Introduction to a Theological Theory of Language* (London: Collins, 1973); and Robert W. Funk, *Language, Hermeneutic and Word of God* (New York: Harper and Row, 1966).

39. Anthony C. Thiselton, *The Two Horizons: New Testament Hermeneutics and Philosophical Description* (Grand Rapids: Eerdmans, 1980), pp. 10-23 et passim.

40. Robert W. Funk, *Parables and Presence* (Philadelphia: Fortress Press, 1982), p. 30; cf. pp. 1-80.

41. Ibid., pp. 88-89.

42. Ibid., pp. 580-81.

43. Ibid.

44. Ibid., p. 638.

45. C. H. Dodd, *Parables of the Kingdom* (London: Nisbet, 1935), p. 16.

46. Robert W. Funk, *Language, Hermeneutic and Word of God,* p. 133.

47. Dodd, *Parables of the Kingdom,* pp. 29-32. Dodd offers two possible interpretations of this parable.

48. Anthony C. Thiselton, "The Parables as Language-Event," *Scottish Journal of Theology,* 23 (1970), 437-68.

49. Joachim Jeremias, *The Parables of Jesus,* 2nd ed. (New York: Scribner, 1963), p. 230.

50. Norman Perrin, *Jesus and the Language of the Kingdom* (London: SCM, 1976), p. 105.

51. Jeremias, *The Parables of Jesus,* p. 120.

52. Perrin, *Jesus and the Language of the Kingdom,* pp. 105-6.

53. Ibid., p. 106.

54. Jeremias, *The Parables of Jesus,* pp. 11-21.

55. Ibid., p. 220.

56. John Sider, "Rediscovering the Parables: The Logic of the Jeremias Tradition," *Journal of Biblical Literature,* 102 (1983), 61-83.

57. Cf. Barthes, "From Work to Text."

58. Nicholas Wolterstorff, *Art in Action* (Grand Rapids: Eerdmans, 1980), p. 125.

59. Ibid., p. 16. Cf. also Nicholas Wolterstorff, *Works and Worlds of Art* (Oxford: Clarendon Press, 1980).

60. In addition to works already cited, cf. Dan Otto Via, *The Parables: Their Literary and Existential Dimension* (Philadelphia: Fortress Press, 1967).

61. In additon to works already cited, cf. Sallie TeSelle, *Speaking in Parables* (Philadelphia: Fortress Press, 1975).

62. Susan Wittig, "A Thing of Multiple Meanings," *Semeia 9* (1977), and Mary

Ann Tolbert, *Perspectives on the Parables* (Philadelphia: Fortress Press, 1979).

63. Crossan, *In Parables,* p. 64.

64. Ibid.

65. Wittig, "A Thing of Multiple Meanings," p. 84.

66. Ibid., p. 86.

67. Ibid., p. 87.

68. John Dominic Crossan, "Finding Is the First Act: Trove Folk Tales and Jesus' Treasure Parable," *Semeia 9* (1977), p. 111.

69. Ibid., pp. 115, 117, and 121.

70. Ibid., p. 139.

71. Richard Rorty, *Philosophy and the Mirror of Nature* (Princeton: Princeton University Press, 1980), p. 356.

72. Fish, *Is There a Text in This Class?* p. 1.

73. Ibid., p. 106.

74. Tolbert, *Perspectives on the Parables,* p. 71.

75. Ibid., p. 39.

76. Ibid., p. 101.

77. Ibid., pp. 101-102.

78. Ibid., p. 104.

79. Ibid., p. 106.

80. Wittig, "A Theory of Multiple Meanings," p. 92.

81. Martin Heidegger, *Holzwege* (Frankfurt: Klostermann, 1950), pp. 22-23, and *Poetry, Language, and Thought* (New York: Harper and Row, 1971), pp. 18-87.

82. Heidegger, *Poetry, Language, and Thought,* p. 40.

83. Martin Heidegger, *On the Way to Language* (New York: Harper and Row, 1971), p. 108.

84. Fuchs, *Hermeneutik,* p. 71; cf. Fuchs's *Studies of the Historical Jesus* (London: SCM, 1964), pp. 91-95 and 141.

85. Ibid., pp. 33-37.

86. Via, *The Parables,* p. 84.

87. J. L. Austin, *How to Do Things with Words* (Oxford: Clarendon, 1962), pp. 101-19.

88. Raymond E. Brown, *The Critical Meaning of the Bible* (New York: Paulist Press, 1981), pp. 23-44.

89. David Couzens Hoy, *The Critical Circle: Literature and History in Contemporary Hermeneutics* (Berkeley: University of California Press, 1978), pp. 11-40.

INDEX

Abrams, Meyer H., 9, 10, 11, 17, 24

aesthetic theory: 6-15; relation to ethical theory, 7; disinterestedness, 7-8, 9, 11, 12, 14, 23, 24, 27; pleasure, delight, 7, 8, 9, 11, 12, 13, 14; Kantian view, 8-11, 14; romantic formalism, 9, 13; imagination, 10-14; relation to American fundamentalism, 23, 24

Ahlstrom, Sydney, 22

allegory: distinguished from parable, 85-86

Althaus, Paul, 28

American cultural hermeneutic: 15-23; Puritan view, 16; Enlightenment view, 16-17; romantic view, 17; relation to American Protestantism, 19-23; Scottish Common Sense Realism, 20-22

Anselm, Saint, 26

Aristotle: *mimesis,* 50, 56

Arnold, Matthew, 32

audience criticism. *See* reader-response hermeneutics

Augustine, Saint, 3-4

Austin, J. L., 6, 83, 95, 107, 109

authorial stance, 69

Bacon, Francis, 5

Baconianism: 4-7, 15-23; relation to

Cartesianism, 5; relation to American cultural hermeneutic, 15-23; relation to American Protestantism, 20-22

Baird, J. Arthur, 90-92

Barth, Karl, 17, 95

Barthes, Roland, 94

biblical interpretation: relation to literary theory, 79-83

Black, Max, 6, 23

Bleich, David, 33

Booth, Wayne, 92-93

Boucher, Madeleine, 90

Bovon, François, 82

Brown, Raymond, 109, 110

Bultmann, Rudolf, 84, 95

Burke, Edmund, 9

Cartesianism: 4-7, 9, 10, 15, 17, 23, 24, 26, 27, 28; relation to Baconianism, 5; relation to romantic theory, 9-10; critique of, 24-29

Chinard, Gilbert, 15

Coleridge, Samuel Taylor, 11, 12

Crèvecoeur, St. John de, 16, 17

Crossan, J. D., 84, 85, 89, 101-5

Culpepper, R. Alan, 92-93

deconstruction. *See* Derrida